Rain *On The*

Red Flag

For Ryan Quam,
I hope you like the book —
Abel Tyyn
Dec 2022 -

FRANK THANH NGUYEN

PAGE PUBLISHING
Conneaut Lake, PA

First originally published by Page Publishing 2022

The stories in this book reflect the author's recollection of events. Some names, locations, and identifying characteristics have been changed to protect the privacy of those depicted. Dialogue has been recreated from memory.

ISBN 978-1-6624-8575-6 (pbk)
ISBN 978-1-6624-8574-9 (digital)

Printed in the United States of America

To my wife, Christine, and my children, Todd and Tyler, whom I love dearly. Without your support and encouragement, I would never have a chance to tell you and the world why and how we are here.

To my father, Nguyen Van Toan, my brother Thach and his family, and my brother Thông, who are looking down from heaven and guided me through the completion of this book.

To all the friends whom I met in jails and labor camps, your bravery, endurance, and courage inspired me to tell this story.

And last but not least, to hundreds of thousands of Vietnamese people who perished at sea seeking freedom.

Tôi bước đi
Không thấy phố,
Không thấy nhà
Chỉ thấy mưa sa
Trên màu cờ đỏ.

I walked alone
There was no town
There was no house
Only rain on the red flag.

—Trần Dần, 1957

ACKNOWLEDGMENT

Thanks to Danielle Wolffe who had worked with me for many years to complete this book. Your kind heart, curiosity, patience, and encouragement enabled me to dig deep into my painful past and bring out the raw truth for the world to see. And thanks to Jay Blotcher, who believed in our work with his whole heart and conviction and helped us to shape up the book.

PROLOGUE

November 1986, Ba Tri, a coastal village, South Vietnam

The first day my father's body washed up in the estuary, the village chief policeman, Phu, noticed. He stuck his wooden pole into my father's side and shoved him back toward the Ba Lai River. The sun bled deep purple over the wide bright green fields, its flatness stretching endlessly toward the blurred horizon.

Phu squatted down on the walkway then looked back to his square brown shrimp farms along the river, watching for the tiny surface bubbles the shrimp made when they popped.

Phu was a kind, gentle man. He had the deep, ruddy sun-washed skin of the coastal people in Ba Tri, a village that curved like a hook in the fluid Mekong Delta and a natural catch point for flotsam. It wasn't unusual for a body to wash up in his yard. For nearly a decade after the official end of the war, the wooden boats of Vietnamese people trying to escape the Communists frequently capsized. Bodies shored like crabs after a storm.

When my father's body washed up again the next day, Phu recognized him—the length of his limbs, the rip on the elbow of his pale blue shirt. He paused. Then he walked out to the end of the wooden walkway, took his long pole, bent at the knees, and gave my father's body another hard push.

Phu watched my father's body for a while, bobbing past the shrimping floats in the brackish water, past the exposed braided roots of his neighbor's mangrove, until it was just a tiny speck. He imagined the body floating on the current down the river, all the way out to the South China Sea.

That night, Phu woke up from a dream. The window was open. Brine coated his throat. In his dream, he had seen my father, the bones of his face exposed.

"Are you awake?" Phu whispered to his wife. He found her cracked hand and squeezed it. She squeezed back. "There was a body today. The same one as yesterday," he whispered.

Phu's wife, a devout Buddhist, didn't respond. It was practically dawn, and she would have to go out to the rice paddy soon. She was a no-nonsense farm woman who worked hard, earning them enough chickens and bitter melon to survive.

Phu nestled closer. Her nightgown clung to the sweat on her plump back. He knew she didn't like to sleep entwined on those hot nights. Still, it brought him comfort to feel her chest rising, to smell the incense in her hair.

On the third day my father's body washed up in Phu's yard, he hooked his pole under my father's shirt and dragged him to shore. He pulled my father into his backyard until he got to his family's cemetery. Phu had decided there was a reason why this man had chosen his backyard. He laid my father on his back and crossed his arms over his chest.

Phu called some friends to help give my father a proper funeral. It took them all day to dig the grave, carefully shoring up the sides and the bottom of the mud with a wall of brick and cement. While it dried and they were preparing my father for burial, Phu found, sewn into a pocket and sealed in plastic, my father's identification card. Our family's address in Saigon was printed on it.

Phu held the card and recited my father's name.

"Nguyễn Văn Tàn," he read. "Toàn," he whispered.

One of Phu's friends, a tall thin man whose face was scarred by childhood acne, noticed my father's sandal was bulging. He bent down and carefully removed the sandal from the water-bloated foot. Sewn inside was a small pouch containing a gold ring.

Phu looked at him sternly.

"We bury him as he came," Phu said.

"He can't use it anymore," the man argued.

Gold had been the currency for the South Vietnamese ever since the Communists took over our city. If my father had been captured again and sent back to the labor camp where he'd been imprisoned for a decade, that one ring could have bought him extra cassava for a month or given him the privilege of contacting us. This ring bound him to my mother, whom he was desperately trying to reach on the other side of that ocean.

Phu turned his back to his friend, a rare gesture for him. Phu was an ethical man whose judgment was well-respected.

"Here, you take care of it then. He's yours," the man said, handing the ring back to Phu. Phu took the ring in his palm and marveled at the green hue the ocean had turned it. Then he put the ring on my father's chest, beneath his folded arms. The men wrapped him tightly in the heavy linen shroud then carefully lowered him into the ground. Phu's wife burned three sticks of incense and led them in chanting.

Weeks passed after my father's body was placed in the family graveyard when something strange started happening. Phu's shrimp farming business took off. At dusk, the shrimp popped in a cacophony of sound that resonated like a Vietnamese opera. Shrimp squirmed heavy on the nets. When he pulled them in, his biceps straining, they were translucent white and the size of a large man's hands. Orders suddenly poured in from everywhere.

Within a month, Phu and his wife had more shrimp than they could handle and enlisted friends to help.

Within a year, they grew incredibly rich. Phu kept his side position as a village policeman, but the family no longer shredded their hands in the paddy. They traded in their humble thatched-roof house for a brick house with electricity, running water, and even an indoor bathroom. Phu bought some extra land along the coast to raise more shrimp.

His wife had rich meat and fish for dinner every night.

Every afternoon at dusk, Phu's wife hiked out to my father's grave. She kneeled and lit an incense stick then prayed, thanking my father for the good fortune that he'd brought them.

Sometimes, Phu watched her, bundled up in her sweater, silhouetted in the shadowy rose light.

He decided to find my father's family.

July 1994

I stared out the window as the plane descended into the airport just outside Saigon, at the maroon rivers twining through the lush green land. My wife, Christine, slept with her head tilted back. I admired Christine's ability to sleep on the plane. I couldn't tune out my thoughts.

I was haunted by a feeling of déjà vu. It wasn't my own memory that cloyed but rather my memory of a short story by Tuong Nang Tien I'd read a decade earlier. The heroine in that story returned to Vietnam long after she'd escaped. At the time the book was written, nobody who escaped Vietnam could imagine returning to our homeland. The fact that it was happening to me then seemed surreal. And I worried what would happen when we landed.

So many emotions flooded my heart. I felt like a river with a blocked drain. My senses remembered how it felt to stand in the lukewarm bathwater air and walk through the clotted market streets in Saigon, to feel the earth give way as we traveled on a ferry over the Mekong River, overripe jackfruit perfuming the air.

But it was no longer the country of my childhood. It had been thirteen years since I'd fled Vietnam. The only thing that was the same were the seasons.

I released another two buttons on the dress shirt I was wearing. I had chosen to look dignified in case we needed to bribe people to leave the airport. I kept reminding myself that I was safe, that I was an American citizen. My frame had thickened. It was no longer the sinew and bone of that starving teenager who spent all day hacking with a machete to harvest corn and cassava in the labor camp. Still, my body remembered. My eyes felt as heavy as they were during those gloomy years, my breathing thin, as if somebody had punctured my chest with a stickpin.

I didn't know who was on the ground awaiting us. The efforts of the US human rights campaigns had shut down the camps, and the iron fist of the Communist had brought stability to the country. But the men who won were our enemies.

We descended. The muddy river was the color of brick, slinking through the green grass. I could make out metal buildings that had looked like thatched houses from higher up.

Suddenly, I didn't want the plane to land.

But then I reminded myself the reason I had returned. I pulled an envelope from my brown leather briefcase. It was the latest of a series of letters from Phu, written in a loping scrawl. I learned it was written by Phu's wife since the peasant lacked formal education.

Dear Mr. Pham van Hung,

We are indebted for the gifts you last sent to us. Our sons loved the American T-shirts and the valuable medications.

We respect your decision to come visit your brother-in-law and bring his remains. We understand. It may be a hard journey. We will do all we can to help in this process.

You are also welcome to visit your brother-in-law any time you wish.

Yours truly,
Phu

I was still unsure we were doing the right thing, taking my father from his resting place to bring him to America. Phu was worried about the exhumation. But he had graced us with a rare gift— evidence of my father's disappearance. We had closure. The families of hundreds of thousands of Vietnamese weren't so lucky. They'd all vanished. Those dead at sea included my eldest brother, Thach, his wife and toddler, six cousins, an uncle and eight other people on their boat, including my old girlfriend and her family.

I refolded the letter, returned it to my briefcase, then leaned back in the seat and shut my eyes.

I tried again to conjure up a memory of my father. I didn't have the chance to get to know him well. I came from a large family and spent most of my time playing with my seven siblings or neighborhood kids. We respected and feared our father, a serious routine-driven military man. It always bothered me that I didn't get to know him as an adult until our last time together. We weren't particularly close. But I had tried.

* * *

The music reverberated through the walls into my brother Thach's room, Thai Thanh's elegant and sorrowful voice belting out "Ky Vat Cho Em" (Memorabilia for You), backed by the deep sound of woodwinds and brass orchestra. My brother smiled. The sweet notes were coming from my father's room. We decided to go visit him.

We sneaked into the room quietly. Our dad was lying on the floor in his pajamas with his head on the pillow. It was rare to see him relaxing, even rarer to see the smile on his face as he listened to the music from a cassette player on the dresser.

I was fourteen years old, and I had to tighten my lips to keep from giggling at the sight of his giant belly bouncing jellylike as he breathed.

Then I got down to lie next to him, my ear resting on his tummy like a pillow. My dad pretended not to notice, but his smile got bigger. We didn't speak. The harmony vibrated through my thighs, and the violin plucks tickled my spine while Thai Thanh's soprano voice echoed through my dad's belly into my ear. This was one of my best memories of my dad. I look back and realize how, as a child, I was seeking a way to get close to him.

* * *

The seat belt lights came on with a ding.

"Are we there?" my wife asked, yawning. She opened her eyes, blinking up at me. She looked beautiful, but like me, she was apprehensive.

I grabbed Christine's hand and gave it a squeeze.

* * *

Faint wind tickled the shocking green fields. Reeds drifted in subtle magnetic waves from one end of the paddy to the horizon. Coconuts and mangroves lined the periphery, loose wobbly trees which belonged neither to the land nor the water.

The place was beautiful but also unsettling. The feeling that I was lost, that I didn't belong there, returned.

Phu walked in front of me. At forty, he was about a decade older than me, but his strong farmer's body navigated the trail without effort.

"Our family is grateful to you. We are forever indebted."

He turned to face me. His skin was dark and ruddy, farmer's wrinkles furrowing the sides of his eyes.

"It is okay," he said simply.

I was in awe of Phu's quiet humility. He continued walking.

With two fingers, I wiped the sludgy sweat that had collected under the white cloth headband the monk had tied to my head. I struggled to keep my footing on the trail, skirting garbage and animal and human waste, the tall grass tickling my bare arms.

The sun hung low in the center of the paddy. It was already noon. We were rushing to complete the exhumation because we had a meeting at the mortuary in Saigon later that day.

Still, I walked slowly. There was a part of me that didn't want to leave that sticky languid place where Phu had saved Dad's body.

"My father was a good man," I started then cleared my throat. "He was always frugal. It drove my mother crazy because she wanted what the other military wives had, like a new car. His frugality probably saved us after the war. At least we had some gold bars to trade."

Phu didn't turn around, but he slowed his pace. He was listening.

"He was in a labor camp for ten years. I was in one too. It bothers me that he managed to survive in that terrible place all those years, just to die in the sea. It doesn't seem fair."

Phu cleared his throat and took a deep breath.

"My brother Thach waited for him to come back. They helped build boats then see others off. They were on the last boat."

Phu turned and stared at me. His eyes filled with sadness before he turned toward the rice paddies. We saw the shrimp fields whose success he attributed to my father.

Phu held the paperwork that allowed for the exhumation of my father's body. His position in Vietnam piqued my curiosity. Like all the villages in the Mekong Delta, Ba Tri had a strange history during the war. Officially, it had been controlled by the South Vietnamese Army. Simultaneously, Vietcong guerrillas would come out of hiding at night and kidnap children, recruiting them for their militia or to act as spies. The farmers had to give up their land. The only people who remained were a famous battalion of elderly people who fought with pickaxes and machetes against both sides to keep their rights to the land.

To maintain his position as a police officer, I suspected he had to cooperate with both opposing sides. He'd probably been some kind of spy for both the Vietcong and the South Vietnamese Army. The village had been a stronghold for Communists, the people responsible for the death of my father, the same people who placed me in the camps and jail.

After the war, they were still controlled by the Communists.

Phu was a simple farmer who'd been caught in the middle.

We'd all lived long enough to recognize that a war never truly exists between the people on the front lines fighting.

Ordinary people are forced to do what is expected of them.

"I know there is a reason my father found this place. Why he wanted to be with your family," I said.

Phu rubbed his chin, and his stoic face twitched slightly, like a dragonfly taking off.

"It brings back memories. Being back. It is strange," I said.

The thick and salty air clung to my newly tanned skin, coating my Adam's apple.

"Could you tell what happened to him? From his body, I mean. Did he drown? Did he have a heart attack? I keep trying to figure out how it happened."

"I don't know that answer," Phu said.

It was quiet on that flat treeless land. But as we got closer to the gravesite, we heard the low chanting of monks and smelled incense.

I was relieved to see my father's grave, nestled in lowland and surrounded by graves of Phu's family. Others were already gathered: Christine, my sister, my uncles, in-law families, and Phu's wife. It was comforting. But still my throat and knees seized as I followed Phu into the gathering.

I was kneeling down, lost in the repetitive beat of the monks chanting, the clanging of the copper cymbals attached to their fingers, the intoxicating incense.

To the right of the gravesite sat traditional plates of tea fruit, rice, and a cooked chicken as an offering to the gods. Candles flickered on silver plates. There were gold bars as well as red and pink paper lanterns, fans, and clothing we would burn to see him off safely.

It was remarkable to me, after all those years in the camp, to see Buddhism practiced again out in the open.

Although we had to wait until Phu had secured the paperwork to officially start the excavation, some mortuary men had started the process, digging a few inches down. They'd exposed the brick and cement wall of my father's grave. I was impressed by the craftsmanship and care. For all those years, he'd been more a part of Phu's family than ours.

Above, a heron screeched on the way to the rice paddy. The monks chanted.

I kept glancing at Phu, noticing a disappointment in his face. He'd treasured his odd relationship with my father. He was wondering what would happen after my father was gone.

Still, he continued to do the right thing. He fought hard until the government released its grip on my father's remains. I was in awe of this man, in awe of his integrity.

xvii

I don't know how long I sat with my head rocking as the monks chanted, preparing my father for departure. But then I heard the sound as the shovel located the first bone.

They uncovered a wristbone that they cleaned off with rice wine. At that point, Christine nudged me, and I bent down in the dusty earth to help. I carried more uncovered bones in the heat, my father's bones—phalanges and toes and his collarbone. I helped to pour the rice wine over the bones in the bucket.

The sweat dripped into my eyes. My throat was as cracked as the earth. My stomach hurt.

Then they found the gold ring—the ring my father had sewn inside his sandal. The ring that Phu had made sure was buried with him. In the back of my mind, I was praying it wasn't him, that there had been some kind of mistake and my dad wasn't dead. It was the prayer of the fourteen-year-old boy using his father's fat tummy as a pillow, feeling the vibrations of Thai Than's soprano vocals in my ears and my legs.

A man passed me a bone he had dug up, and I held it, surprised by its lightness. It was an arm bone. It wasn't hollow like the others. Inside was a platinum rod from when he'd broken his arm in the army.

It was him. My father. We finally knew.

My vision grew blurry as I passed the arm to the man who put it in the bucket and another poured rice wine from a jug.

I don't know how long we sat there, clawing in the dirt, the sun beating on my neck, the sweat pouring down from my headband. I kept helping, my gut clenching deeper and deeper as we dug, as we placed bones in a bucket to be cleaned with wine. I couldn't breathe right. I was afraid I would vomit.

After it was over, I sat down with my legs pulled into my chest, writhing and sobbing deep childlike sobs. Chills traveled down my neck and my spine, all the way to the back of my knees, feeling like blades of grass on the rice paddy, waving with the wind. The tears kept coming.

I looked around and realized I wasn't the only one.

We stood near the hearse as they loaded the casket with my father's bones. The sun had lowered some. Christine and my sister were in the back seat, waiting. I was worried we wouldn't make it to the mortuary in Saigon in time for them to accept the bones for cremation.

My eyes were swollen. Ash from the offerings we'd burned, to make sure my father's spirit went where it was supposed to, clung to my hair and my clothes. My stomach was still bloated from the blessed food that we ate. But there was something intoxicating about standing there, the air acrid-sweet with salt and coconut. I didn't want to move.

Phu stood, looking at the hearse. He would miss him. The gift he gave us would cost him.

In the hazy sunlight, I briefly looked at Phu's features—the wide plane of his cheekbones and his ruddy skin, the way he squinted his eyes.

"We are forever indebted to you," I said.

Phu's expression, which had been veiled for most of the day, suddenly changed. His eyes grew watery. He took my hand and shook it firmly. We held each other's gaze.

It was a senseless time, his eyes said. *We did what we could.*

CHAPTER 1

We Have to Go

April 29, 1975, Saigon

I looked at my eldest brother, Thinh, standing in front of the main room, smoothing his too long hair from his eyes. I saw what nobody else could. The quiet was bothering him. Martial law had been declared a few days before, and the city was silent. Our streets, usually filled with songs blasting from kitchen radios and market stands, were bereft of music.

Thinh had hung out at coffee shops where the hippie kids listened to Vietnamese anti-war music, Trinh Cong Son's protest tunes, and sad acoustic love songs that plucked at your heart. They'd all been closed down. Many of his friends were fleeing the city.

"Where did you see them all going again, Thinh?" I asked.

Thinh looked toward my mother, sitting in a chair, her makeup perfectly applied over her pale face. She was wearing a formal green-colored ao dai, a long silk tunic dress over trousers.

My mother's hand shook as she lifted a cold teacup to her lips.

Thinh was wearing the dirt-caked pants he had put on to ride his scooter through the city and look for news. His forehead cinched with discomfort. He was faced with the obligations of eldest brother, a role that fit him awkwardly.

"Why?" he answered.

"I am just curious," I said.

"They are going down Tran Quoc Toan Street, Nguyen Van Thoai Street. Those are the only places left where you can avoid the checkpoints."

"How are they traveling?" my younger brother, Thông, asked. Thông had ruddy brown skin. We all teased him because he didn't resemble anyone in our family. He was a sweet boy who followed me around. "How?" he asked. His tone was aggravated.

"Anyway they can. On foot. By bike. By car and scooter."

"Stop worrying. We are fine," Thach said. He was one year older than me.

Thach was like Thinh in that he didn't care about school. My parents considered him lazy. But Thach had a kind of moral strength my parents didn't understand. I envied this. Despite his good looks, he wasn't a playboy like Thinh. Instead, he had the same pretty girl-friend since middle school. He had the same popularity and con-fidence as Thinh, but his social circle was diverse, not like Thinh's largely wealthy friends. Thach socialized with everyone, from the junkies in the slums to cultured people in the wealthiest part of town.

It made me feel safe to hear Thach talking. He was the one who could help us the most. Thach had a talent that my parents previously considered a handicap. He was able to blend wherever he went. It was the first time in his life this questionable skill provided something valuable to our family.

The rest of the kids were unusually calm. Two of the youngest were trading cartoon cards in the living room. They were all restless because my brother had called them in from a soccer game.

"How long will we wait?" I asked Thinh.

My mother stared up at him.

"You kids must pack," Thinh said.

Thông sat by the younger kids. He looked up from a game of Chinese checkers on the square-shaped wooden board. The young ones' eyes were wide. They seemed to nestle closer together.

We didn't really think about what it meant to leave our home behind for America. We knew we had to escape Saigon because the Communists were moving in. We pictured the Communists as nasty barbarians on a killing spree. We didn't think too much harder about it than that. Our parents had gotten upset after listening to radio reports of the South collapsing, how we had lost one city after another, how refugees escaping were dying on boats.

"Are the children all packed?" my mother asked Thinh.

We didn't have anything to pack. We each had a small sack with dry food and fruits. We were wearing the only clothes we were allowed to take. They were uncomfortable because my mother had sewn heavy gold bars into the children's socks and underpants.

Inside my sack, I had a small address book listing my relatives and classmates. It made me sad to hold it.

"We cannot take any cassette tapes, Thanh," Thinh said.

There was a sadness to his expression. Everyone in our family loved music, but Thinh was obsessed. He shared this passion only with me.

When Thinh babysat, he used to make us take naps. Then he cranked up the phonograph with his favorite records. I remembered being ten years old, lying on the mat with my eyes closed, when the heavy beat of rock and roll washed over me, the music brought by American soldiers, like the Rolling Stones, CCR, Jimi Hendrix. It flooded from my hip bone and thigh, curled in the fetal position to my chest, where I held my fist.

The moment I shared with Thinh stuck with me. Our closeness was through music exclusively. I thought about my five-string acoustic guitar, its weight when I held it in my lap, the way I could feel it in my whole body when I played.

Thinh was pacing again, peeking through the shades to the empty streets.

I wondered if there was more to the story, something my brother hadn't yet told us.

That night, the silence was broken by shelling that was so close we could feel it, shocking our hearts where we lay. The beat of helicopter blades and voices of evacuees from the TV rose and fell like ocean waves on a beach.

I lay awake, my duffle bag on my bed already packed.

I'd always been an orderly boy and didn't question rules, trusting that the world made sense. But I thought about the small freedoms we were losing. I would not take the high school exit exams. I'd never work up the courage to talk to Mai, that cute girl I sat behind in an English class with her short skirt and her glossy black hair styled in a demi-garcon smelling like berries.

We couldn't even go outside.

"What is taking our father so long? Why hasn't he given us the signal?" I whispered.

I was too young to sit in on the family meetings but had eavesdropped. My uncle Quy, a military helicopter pilot for the vice president, was stationed on a base near the Tan Son Nhat Airport, on the outskirts of Saigon. We'd meet him somewhere after a signal. He'd take us to the airport base to evacuate.

I didn't know where we were going from there.

Things must have been getting bad because usually, my dad didn't trust his younger brother-in-law. My uncle was a typical young pilot, reckless and obsessed with his physical prowess. He was too liberal and a womanizer. Ironically, I spent more time with him than with Dad. He would take us out to the horse racetrack nearby and taught us how to use rifles and handguns to shoot sparrows.

I got out of bed and walked to the main room. My mother and eldest brother were sitting there silently, two cups of coffee in front of them. The green curtains were drawn, but something bright flickered behind them.

My brother shook his leg and picked a zit on his forehead. My mother's mouth was screwed shut. They'd been having another disagreement.

"No signal yet?" I asked, stunning them both.

My mother stared at the curved wooden edge of the couch.

"Mom, we should go while it's still dark. Before martial law is enforced," my brother said. "The military police are gathering in certain spots," he continued. "They are manning checkpoints and focusing on cars because everyone is trying to get out."

He explained the route to the hospital, ten miles away, and how we should collect our extended family members and load all the bicycles and scooters.

"Let's just go there because we don't know what's going on. Later, it could be difficult to get through the streets," he said.

An hour later, my mother finally agreed.

4

CHAPTER 2

Secret Landing Zone

The hospital was buzzing with desperate people. They sat with their kids and belongings in the lobby. Men stood in stairwells. Women squatted in front of mats, feeding children boiled eggs and pickled vegetables.

Overnight, people had decided the hospital was the safest place in the city. The modern five-floor building was a fortress. After all, it was the place where they always came after their bodies had endured other attacks, and it was a place to heal.

"We will be okay."

"The South Vietnamese Army is still on the streets."

"They aren't winning."

The conversations wafted through the hallways smelling of disinfectant and fear.

I glanced at the clusters of unsettled people around me. Most of the adults' facial expressions were unreadable, in keeping with our cultural etiquette of not showing strong emotion. People prayed quietly, lips barely moving, fingers turning prayer beads.

It was impossible to define what was happening. There was no reason to rely on, no letters to shape into words. The situation was completely outside our realm of experience.

There were nearly twenty-five members of my family at the hospital. We ranged in age from my mom at forty-five to my pregnant aunt's three-month-old baby in her arms. We were a large clumsy group. The children wore heavy layers of clothing. I wondered if we would all be able to fit on the copter, or if our heavy bones and luggage would cause it to sink, like a ship.

"We should peek in on the fourth floor," Thinh joked. There were rumors that the fourth floor was reserved only for the president and his relatives.

"You boys stop being foolish," one of my uncles snapped.

"It's not a bad idea. Let's head up," said my other uncle Hieu.

We surged as one group, bombarding the stairwell. But a guard wearing a blue uniform began scolding us.

"You can't go up there. It isn't safe."

"We have no interest in the fourth floor."

"Just let us through. We won't bother you."

The guard seemed scared and moved his body closer to my uncles, as if this would block us. He was in a terrible position, trying to keep nervous people contained as the fighting rolled into the city. Desperation tugged his vocal cords.

"I can't allow this."

I slipped between my relatives in the stairwell and found a spot near the wall.

Loud and angry male voices echoed in the cool stairwell. Then the voices dropped off. I strained to understand. There was a loud grinding sound coming from above. The copter was really close.

Thinh was in front of the guard. He signaled to me with his chin to sneak up to the roof, our secret landing zone. I hiked my duffle bag on my shoulder, separating from the sweaty bodies of my nieces and nephews.

As my brother argued extra loudly, I ran up to the third floor then the fourth. My normally polite family raised their voices behind me.

I reached the fifth floor. I started to open the heavy metal door, but the wind slammed it shut. I braced my body against it, forcing it open. I made it through and planted my feet in the ground, bending low to gain gravity.

I let my eyes fall on the view surrounding me. Smoke billowed up behind the domed airport building. On the street below, no civilians remained. Only tanks and green hulking soldiers with guns sticking out of their armpits. They blocked the streets, a herd of strange animals with raised tusks.

The helicopter hovered about fifty feet away. It was a Huey. I had learned to recognize it from my uncle. Its dark green body looked like a grasshopper. Its thump-thump-thumping sound echoed in my blood. He had explained that over seven thousand army Hueys had flown in our country during the war. Every time my uncle wanted to show off a new type of helicopter, he'd fly it over our house. He'd fly low, training the glow of his headlights on us. We cheered and jumped up and down as he passed. I remembered the day he flew the Huey over our house.

I ran across the rooftop. My uncle had a Huey. I took off my pale blue shirt and waved it, running bare chested toward the helicopter.

"Uncle Quy!" I tried to scream. "Here, Uncle Quy. It's me, Thanh!"

The helicopter circled close, and I expected my uncle to land and open the door to the cockpit. I'd explain how the rest of the family was trapped by the guard in the stairwell.

"Uncle Quy!"

The copter had come so close that the wind stirred up my hair, as if it was being pulled by the roots. Then it veered to the left and left the hospital roof. I went to the edge of the rooftop and watched it descend like a bird until it landed in a patch of land, a high school field, just beyond a row of houses. A big family of dozens of people ran toward the copter.

I got back down the stairs, my stomach sloshed. My heart thumped in my skinny chest. My uncle Hieu was getting upset. His eyes were intense. He reached down and pulled something from his bag. My uncle was holding a gun behind his back. The guard couldn't see it.

I waved my arms in the air and screamed, "No, that's not Uncle Quy! The helicopter was not ours. It is gone."

My angry uncle never looked at me, but he heard me. One of the women in my family moaned, and another started chanting. The expression on my uncle's face changed. He nodded and tucked his gun back into his pants.

CHAPTER 3

The Fall of Saigon

We camped out in that second-floor stairwell all night, making little nests for ourselves. The youngest children curled into their mothers, occasionally drinking water and eating dry instant noodles. I closed my eyes, and their voices weaved in and out of my dreams.

I woke up, choking on stuffy air. The guard was no longer there. A small window cast eerie smoked silver light on some of the children's faces. Uncle Hieu stood near the cracked ventilation shaft, watching the airport. The pop-pop-popping sound of the shelling continued low staccato hum.

"Come see," my uncle whispered, waving toward me.

I stood up, dizzy and dehydrated. My chest ached from the way I'd been curled all night. When I reached the shaft, I stood up on the balls of my feet on the stairs and squinted to look through the arm-sized crack in the shaft.

I gasped. The sky was a greenish gray color that didn't seem like day or night. Long columns of smoke billowed everywhere.

"The American Marine Corps launched an evacuation," Uncle Hieu explained. "There are convoys of helicopters, huge ones."

"I think those are the Sea Stallion carriers that come from the US fleets," said Thinh, who came to join us.

The sky flashed with light from one of the helicopters. It swooped down near the airport and then kept going.

"That one didn't land at the airport," I said.

"No, there are meeting points, secret ones. They are getting orders from the CIA, the American government, far away."

"So they are here to help?" I asked.

"I don't know," my uncle said, a despondent tone in his voice.

"Depends on strategy. They could be here to get their own people, maybe rescue some of our high-ranking officials."

Helicopters emerged from the murky gray soup. They lit the undercarriage of clouds, a shiny alien light. I turned back toward the stairwell.

It was strange to see my whole family sprawled out so informally like that, their normally delicate clothing rumpled on their bodies. The belongings were packed in between everyone or being used as backrests or pillows, and there seemed to be more of them than people. It reminded me of nights when we used to have parties, gathering with the help in the kitchen, women talking about housework and men sipping coffee. There was something about the familiarity that made the night feel safer somehow.

The stairwell had become a trap. Hours stretched. We were no longer trying to sleep, our family squished together. Women listlessly combed the hair of small children held between their legs. We had become attuned to the rhythm of bombs exploding in the distance. People tried to adjust their conversations to the explosions, but there was no way to anticipate the interruptions. We reasoned that the bombing and shelling could only go for so long before people had to stop, before the street had to rest. My legs twitched with restlessness. Hunger gnawed at my belly. I was tired of sitting in that stairwell. If I didn't get up soon, I would scream.

I tapped Thinh on the arm and indicated I wanted to go over to the shaft. He was quiet, his expression unreadable. Then he looked at his watch and slowly nodded.

The city already resembled a nightmare, a place I did not recognize. People no longer existed. The navy blue sky was smudged with a gray film. The mortar had been dropped to explode, one after the other, until they reached the central capital and Presidential Palace.

An explosion occurred, and I stood there, holding the ledge with my fingers. I no longer flinched. It now fascinated me. I had always been good at math. I counted the amount of time it took between each explosion. Nobody bothered me. I watched for so long that I was able to predict where and when the next one would occur. Each time I guessed, I was right.

Eventually, I looked back at my family crouched in the stairwell, their faces undefinable in the shadows. I quietly slipped up the stairs and stopped at the top, my heart beating so hard I could feel it in my hips and my knees. The door opened easily, and I slipped out to the roof.

I stood there, breathless and smiling. It was a brisk April morning. The streets were filled with clouds of soft mist. I'd never really stayed up all night and hadn't seen the world at that hour. It was magical. I crab-walked toward the edge of the rooftop. I examined the street that led to the Presidential Palace. It was quiet. Nobody was awake.

The left side of the street was like a large village, tiny one- or two-story houses knitted side by side. The mist had pooled there and was lifting in the small patches of lawn, ordinary rectangular shapes. They seemed miniature, so strange.

It was only then that I noticed the red flags stuck on the front door of each house.

Those were the Communist flags. Each of those houses with tiny lawns had been claimed. Our city was no longer ours.

Dizziness hit me, and I sat down, pushing my forehead against the cool stone wall.

Slowly, I stood up again. Down below, a gnarled tank which had been blasted was burning. What I thought had been mist was smoke.

Further down the street, I saw soldiers in green clothing carrying guns. There were more fires on the street, made from piles of rubber truck tires.

I sat back down. It was too unbelievable to take in.

I'd never thought the Communists would take over.

I ran back downstairs to tell my family.

CHAPTER 4

Run, Run, Run

My family stood on the wide street in front of the hospital. It was the same street we'd watched being shot up. Nobody was on it. Guns and uniforms littered the ground.

We had decided to try and go back home.

My pregnant aunt stood beside me, holding the hands of some of the nephews. Thach was one of the bigger kids, so he had one of the youngest children on his back, a heavy boy who kept grabbing his neck and giggling. He almost choked. It was difficult to balance him and the bag on Thach's shoulder. I reached back, found his small fingers, and loosened them.

The silence outside was dangerous. We walked across the street slowly. The air was hot and stuffy. My family was wobbly, knobby-kneed, our belongings weighing us down.

The boy poked his sticky fist in Thach's eye, and shots rang out.

We moved quickly off the main street, onto crooked side alleys. The sunlight stung, and it was hard to see where we were going. When we finally stopped, we'd accidentally split up into two groups.

"We should wait for them."

"We will be vulnerable. We cannot stop for long."

"We will get shot."

Thach reached back and tickled the boy's side. He giggled.

"Besides, they will keep going too."

"He's right."

"Okay then, let's go."

We walked, navigating the narrow and broken little streets. The windows of the houses were shuttered, doors locked. We were the only ones on the street.

There was no way to tell if we were circling farther away or closer to our own neighborhood. We were lost.

This was the only city I had ever known. Suddenly, it was unfamiliar.

We stopped in an alley so narrow it could only fit three people side by side.

My pregnant aunt had her head tilted back, resting on stone. The sun exposed the strain on her skin. She was holding the cup of a thermos. Children stood around her, waiting for their turn.

Someone called out, and I looked down. Discarded South Vietnamese uniforms, shirts, pants, and helmets lay on the ground.

Where were the bodies that had worn this clothing? Had they been stripped naked and shot?

"Surrendered," one of my uncle's mumbled.

Nobody had thought to bring a radio from the hospital. There was no way we could have known that at ten that morning, as we were stumbling through the alleys, the president had resigned. The new president ordered an issue for the South Vietnamese Army to surrender.

That was why the soldiers had stripped off their identifying clothing before leaving.

We had lost.

My brother Thinh had a friend Long. His house was in a slum. The scent of fish heads, urine, and metal wafted from the broken streets. Sadness stretched and hung like clothing in the heavy air.

It was a crime-ridden neighborhood. Residents had become adept at being invisible. Small ramshackle houses cut into apartments held two or three large families. The windows were shuttered.

My exhausted family stood in a tight group, as if that would keep us all standing up. The sun beat down. Sweat rolled into our eyes, blurring our vision. The stench of our dirty sweat assaulted us. A black jeep rolled slowly down the street. There were male and female civilians in the back, people from Saigon that had been captured. There were both men and women on the truck, their faces stripped of sound. A red flag was attached to the antennae.

It passed. We didn't look up. But then we heard someone coming. It was Long's father.

He saw my brother and led us toward his house. We followed the man silently down the dingy streets. We followed the man as he unlatched the gate to his small house.

"Welcome," said the mother. She was wearing a simple housedress and had hair that bobbed at her shoulders. She stood at the stove, filling plates for us. She invited us to sit down.

Thinh and his lanky friend smirked at each other, the way my brother did when he was in trouble. For a second, embarrassment flushed Thinh's face, a rare expression for him. I watched them sneak off to a corner and start chatting.

I squatted down on the floor near the kids around a makeshift low table as the mother started setting down plates. My pregnant aunt's hand shook as she began eating. My eyelids fluttered.

"You must be hungry. It is only simple fermented soybeans and rice. Please enjoy them," she said, handing bowls, spoons, and chopsticks to the kids.

My family gratefully slurped their food. I looked at my bowl and suddenly realized how hungry I was.

Long was a true friend. His family was poor, but they didn't hesitate to let us in and. They were sharing their only food, the food the poorest families ate.

I picked up the spoon and shoveled a mound in my mouth. It was so hot and rich and good, with spices like garlic and soy. Everything was perfect—the fluffy consistency of rice, the stewed gravy, and the firm beans.

It was one of the best meals I ever had.

CHAPTER 5

The Communists

We returned to our neighborhood as the sun was setting. If anyone saw us, they might have thought we'd been out a long time. Our sweaty clothing stuck under our armpits and backs, making us itch. We craved sleep more than anything.

I stood staring at the familiar houses with wide stone walkways and flowers. They didn't seem real. Everything had changed overnight. The world we'd left behind was gone.

"Let me check to see if the house is there," Thinh said.

Life had shifted for my brother overnight. He'd become the one trusted to guide us.

As I watched him disappear down the street, the ring of sweat on the back of his white shirt, I thought about how natural the leadership role had suddenly become to him after all those years he'd spent waffling along on the streets that had been preparing him for this, how maybe there was some greater thing he'd been destined for that we couldn't understand.

It struck me then how that contrasted with my own life, all those careful ruined plans.

We stood across from the row of concrete houses. Truck tires rolled down distant streets. The longer I waited, the more devastated I felt, and the more aware of how ill-equipped I was to deal with what was happening. I stood there, numb and mute, waiting for Thinh to come back and tell us what we should do.

Thinh returned twenty minutes later. The way he was smiling was strange.

"The house is still there. But the neighborhood is a mess. The street where we live is okay. But in the slum, those little pickpockets seem to have decided they're Communists now."

He breathed hard, his breath thick and mucusy.

"They got ahold of a red cloth and tied it on their arm like a bandage. And they picked up the abandoned guns, and they are trying to take over the whole city now."

He laughed in an incredulous way.

"I was trying to get to our house. At first, those little punks wouldn't let me go. But they know me. They know me. I laughed at them, and I reminded them I am a friend of their older brothers. So they finally let me pass." Thinh laughed again. "The house is fine. But our father isn't there. We should go back to the hospital. Let's take the scooters because we don't want to lose them."

I rode on the back of bike of my brother's friend, watching the streets that had filled with North Vietnamese tanks. They had occupied the majority of the city. The tanks were manned by young boys, their bodies skinny and puny. They also stood on the streets in their uniforms. They weren't cheering their victory. They were quiet, confused.

Later, we found out that the Communist Army didn't expect to win so quickly, that the United States would withdraw. The Army of the Republic of Vietnam had collapsed in a few months without American military aid. The young soldiers had been brainwashed to believe they had come in to liberate the South.

My brother's friend drove us to the hospital parking lot, which had been occupied by tanks and military trucks since we left. North Vietnamese soldiers were stalking the building.

We walked quickly, skirting along the shadow of the concrete barriers until we got to the garage, where we had locked our scooters. They were still there.

My brother and I hopped on our Suzuki scooters and started to pull out, but we were quickly surrounded by a group of young soldiers.

15

We stopped. They showered us with questions on the bikes and how they worked. It was hard to understand their Northern accent, at first. They wore ragged uniforms that looked like big brother hand-me-downs. Their sandals were made from truck tires. These were poor child soldiers from the villages, forced to live and fight in the jungle. Just as I had never been out of Saigon, they had never been far from home. They looked at the city as if it was outer space.

"Oh, it's a scooter."

A few of them walked around the scooter, examining it. One patted it. I sat there, feeling foolish, doubting they would jump me to steal it. My brother didn't think they were dangerous either.

I showed them how the key worked, how the clutch worked. They were very polite, and they kept laughing.

These kids are not the Communists, I thought. Mean adult men with severe haircuts never smiled.

They asked me for a test ride politely, but I had to shake my head.

"I would, but we have to get home and see our father," I said, smiling reluctantly.

They thanked me for showing them the bike. They were just happy lighthearted kids.

CHAPTER 6

Coffee Stand

In the plum-colored night, the air was especially sweet. We sat on low blue stools at the coffee stand. The tables were dingier than before the occupation, and there were fewer streetlamps on. But these were the most comfortable hours to be outside. The soldiers couldn't afford to buy anything from our shops. Occasionally, they performed night maneuvers and moved through the streets stealthily, but mostly, they camped out and laughed quietly or slept. Sometimes I felt sad for them, imagined their uneasiness in what to them was a strange and opulent city, their yearning to return home.

"They took my neighbor," a friend said in a quiet voice, his mouth barely moving.

"Why?"

"They called his name already. He was hiding out. Failure to report."

We were wearing American dungarees. We had an elevated sense of importance because everything we had been taught to believe in had been lost. Everything that defined success for us in the past only served to confine us. We were no longer expected to go to university or get married to good girls. Our only responsibilities were to escape and survive.

We were just as likely to die in the future as we were to escape. The present was the only thing we had.

This awareness heightened everything.

"I saw them," he said.

Nobody responded. We'd all heard the stories of the Secret Police in their yellow uniforms, coming to homes, taking away a guy in the jeeps, and disappearing into the night. We didn't know what happened to them.

"They were quiet. That was strange," he said.

The streets were nearly deserted. The man at the coffee stand picked a small silver pot off the stove then poured steaming liquid into tiny white ceramic cups.

"They are taking junkies too."

A cyclo passed, the driver pushing pedals on the three giant wheels, carrying a woman in the seat in front of him.

"I hear there are camps they are putting them in. Like prisons."

It was just barely raining. The streetlamps cast an eerie glow. We were cold.

An old man with thick gray hair stood in front of the coffee stand. The vendor ladled some coffee into his cup. The old man's wrists were thin and strained when he lifted the cup. He stood up tall, though. He leaned toward the vendor to tell him a story. His voice was low and his expression gentle. Like us, he was relieved by the fresh air and conversation.

When I find myself in times of trouble, Mother Mary comes to me...

Lines from the Beatles tune "Let It Be" ran through my mind.

Speaking words of wisdom, let it be, let it be.

We weren't allowed to listen to the Beatles anymore. Most good music, everything Western, French, even love songs from our region were now called *yellow music*, and they had been banned.

We could only listen or play in secret.

And when the broken people living in the world agree, there will be an answer...

"Are you guys all coming to Minh's house tonight?" I asked.

Let it be...let it be. Let it be. Let it be. There will be an answer...

"Are you?" Chan asked.

Chan was not wearing American dungarees like the rest of us, and he'd cut his hair short because he was trying to pass as a good citizen. Chan was a few in our group whose parents weren't connected to the military. The rest of us boys no longer had any chance to be accepted into university in Vietnam. Chan, the least studious but smartest one among us, could get in.

If he went to school, he wouldn't be drafted into the Youth Corps, traveling throughout the country to do volunteer work, clearing jungles or working in rice paddies. He was going to live.

The old man had taken a seat. His eyes crinkled. He regarded the night—streetlamp, cracked pavement, us boys sitting together. He smiled slightly as if he was reading a pleasant tale.

"Sure," I said.

Minh's house was cozy, a private place to talk all night. His parents left us alone.

We finished our coffee and left the cups on the tables. One boy pulled out a pack of cigarettes.

"You guys want a smoke?"

Each of the guys pulled a cigarette from the pack. I had never held a cigarette before.

I watched as each guy put the cigarette in his mouth while the other lit it within a cupped hand, and it glowed like a lantern in Chinatown. I watched each chest rise as they sucked in the cigarette and let out the smoke. I was careful to take a small pull so I didn't cough and embarrass myself.

I started to crave the taste of the smoke, the way that it burned. I was sucking harder. Eventually, I got a little dizzy.

Warm steam rose from the coffee seller's stand. More people had gathered on the low stools.

I took another long drag off my cigarette, wishing the night wouldn't end.

The next day, my mother came into the room with a pot of coffee and poured some into my dad's cup. He looked at her, and a softness passed between them. It was only the afternoon, but my dad looked exhausted.

During normal times, my dad would come to breakfast in his uniform every morning at eight. Then he would wait for his driver to pick him up. It was already noon, typically the time when his driver dropped him off for lunch. Instead, he was drinking his third cup of coffee.

"Do you want some, Thanh?" my mother asked awkwardly.

It had been three weeks since Saigon had fallen. My father had been a high-ranking official, a lieutenant colonel in the Army of the Republic of Vietnam. The threat to his safety was like a gas leak. We couldn't see it or smell it or do anything to keep it from spreading through the house. They would come for him eventually.

"So how did my grandma disappear?" I asked.

For three weeks, I'd been sitting with Dad in the mornings, listening to stories about his life growing up and our family. There was a practical reason for his stories. He was trying to fill all the drawn-out hours.

My dad took a sip of his coffee then gently put it down on the coffee table. There was a deliberateness about every movement now.

"This was just after World War II, remember. The French had been fighting to control Vietnam against the Communist party, then the Viet Minh. The Viet Minh wanted independence from the colonizers. We lived in the North, in Ha Noi. We were Nationalists. The Nationalists didn't want anything to do with the Communists, but they also wanted independence from the French.

"Things got bad fast. Everyone was running, trying to escape. At the time, your grandparents had a house in the city and a pharmacy in town, Hai Phong. Sometimes, he stayed in town to work in the pharmacy, and your grandma lived at the house. When the war broke out, it was just like now. Chaos, confusion. They both fled. He lost contact with her. But your grandfather, he loved her so much. He tried to find her. He talked to people and tried to figure it out."

"How could they get separated so quickly?"

My dad looked at his large hands in his lap, as if they didn't belong to him.

"Eventually, he found out that she was able to get on a ferryboat headed to another town, but the boat capsized. She drowned. The loss devastated him. More than any other loss that followed.

"In 1954, France surrendered to the Communist-ruled Viet Minh. Vietnam was split into the two halves, the North and the

South through the Geneva Convention. Ngô Đình Diệm became Prime Minister of Nationalist South Vietnam, and Ho Chi Minh became president of Communist North Vietnam. And Nationalists in the North were allowed to take refuge in the South. So we did that, along with two million other people.

"Your grandfather had lost everything—the pharmacy, his house, his wife, his standing in society, his friends. And he was so sad. I remember watching him. He'd do nothing but play mahjong all day and night. He sat so long and got hemorrhoids. He had so much internal bleeding but didn't get treatment and eventually died."

My father took a sip of the cold coffee. Then he left the room.

CHAPTER 7

The Liberators

The sun was beginning to set. I stood in the shade of an awning, my bicycle against my hip. The cold water in the shower had been enough to scrape the dirt off. My hair was combed with the part to the side.

I took a deep breath, inhaling the scent of woodsmoke, and bougainvillea. The world outside my dark house was getting stranger. But I was sick of being stuck in my room all day, reading Chinese serial stories. My parents had considered them frivolous, and I was usually forbidden to read them. They didn't mind anymore because there was no more school or schoolwork.

I wiped the sweat from my forehead with the back of my hand.

In the distance, the Communist music blared—demented upbeat Victorian tunes coming from a few blocks away in the white villa that was formerly owned by a congressman. The Communists had rigged a loudspeaker in a tree to blare their propaganda broadcasts.

"The GDP is rising like never before. The successful fifty percent increase on the production line supersedes our targeted goals. The country has regained its workforce. Everyone is relieved that they have a place that is likely to..."

From the shadow of the tree, I watched North Vietnamese soldiers who had built an encampment behind my house. My neighbors, the families who used to live in those houses, a widow with her kids, were gone. Some had escaped as the city was falling. It was strange to see the houses transformed like that, to imagine the

22

unused furniture and kitchen utensils, the shuttered windows, unoccupied rooms behind locked doors.

All down the row were houses like these, where people we used to see on the street every day no longer lived. Some had escaped as the city was falling. Others were among those we saw being taken away.

Those of us left in Saigon lived like ghosts.

The soldiers that had set up camp were just skinny boys, like the ones in the hospital parking lot. They barely spoke, and when they did, their voices did not resemble the authoritarian voices from the loudspeaker.

As I stood there watching the young soldiers, I was practically invisible. It fascinated me how they lived so primitively. There were about fifteen assigned to each house. They kept their guns and supplies inside. Some slept inside. The encampment had an outdoor stove made of brick. Piles of firewood chopped from the houses were stacked beside it. There was a huge metal cooking pot over the fire, steam rising, the scent of rice and overboiled vegetables filling the air. I noticed that they rarely had meat. Among their most prized possessions was a water canteen each took good care of.

I was surprised at how somber they were, their lives muted as if they were living underwater. The music was a ruse. These guys never celebrated their victory. Instead, they sat for long periods, practically inert. But they never seemed bored.

The soldiers' schedule was repetitive. Every morning, they woke at dawn and ate rice. Then they did military exercises. Then they rested. At lunchtime, they stood in line to get rice. The morning routine repeated.

It was free time now, and my favorite time to watch them. Two boys were washing their clothes in big tubs and hand drying them over a line. Two more were squatting in a shady corner, playing a board game with chips and moving pieces. I marveled at how they lived in the city as if they were at camp in the jungle.

At this time of day, they were taught a class about Communism. I saw how blindly they obeyed orders. At the same time, they were boys like me, probably unable to avoid the draft by studying. They had been duped too. They had been told they were coming to the South to be heroes, to liberate a poor country that had been colonized by the Americans. They had no idea their real purpose was to expand Communism throughout Southeast Asia, that the war was being driven by China and the USSR.

A few boys squatted in the dirt, eating rice from bowls. One looked up, and I was sure he saw me. He remained quiet.

That was how it was between us. We didn't talk to each other. We didn't try to get to know each other. At the same time, we didn't hate each other. They had a kind of begrudging respect for us. They had come to liberate us, but we had richer lives and freedom than any of them.

CHAPTER 8

The Last Moment

I knelt in my parents' bedroom, carefully lifting two loose tiles from the floor. I reached my hand in and pulled out some gold bars. After I replaced the tiles, I went to the kitchen and handed my mom the gold bars. My father nodded his approval.

That afternoon, a radio station had announced that all former government workers and military personnel needed to register at a center. They said the men would be kept a few days to learn about new policies. Of course, we knew this was a lie. But my dad had to report. If he tried to flee, our family would be in danger.

I tried to think about other things. Later that night, I was supposed to go to the coffee stand to meet my friends.

"Sit, Thanh," my dad said.

I sat in my usual spot.

"I loved my father," he said. "I respected him a lot. He built a successful business from scratch at a time when politics made that difficult. When I first became an army officer, our family was so poor. Do you remember when we were living in Da Lat? You were so young. I think you were five when we moved to Saigon. I was able to buy a house."

My mother sat down near my father. Her hand was so close to his hand.

"And we did okay. From that empty hand, your mother and I were able to build up a life, and we raised our eight children. You had clothes. We never went hungry."

"But no car," my mother said. They both laughed.

"Your mother may have faulted me for being so frugal. But I was saving up to spare you. I knew that one day, the money would help you."

My mother moved her arm closer to my father. It was a rare gesture of intimacy. I recognized the enormity of what was happening. My father would probably not be coming home.

Without realizing what I was doing, I took a cigarette out of the pocket of my jeans pants. I lit it.

My dad had been a heavy smoker his whole life, but he didn't believe young people should smoke.

I don't know why I lit the cigarette. Maybe it was my way of showing him that I had grown up, that I could take care of myself.

"I'm sorry, Thanh," my dad said, disappointed.

I took a slight drag of the cigarette so I didn't have to answer him.

"That things turned out like this. You had such dreams. We made so many plans."

I watched the cigarette smoldering, trying to figure out where to flick the ash.

"You were the smart one. You were going to go to college. Become a doctor."

It was never my dream to become a doctor. But I studied hard the way I was supposed to. I did know that studying abroad at a Western college was the only way of being successful, aside from the military.

"He will go one day," my mother said.

"Yes," my dad agreed.

He stared at the tip of my lit cigarette, then looked away

A week later, my mother stood in the kitchen packing a basket with my father's favorite foods, like dried shredded pork. It was a small gesture of comfort she was offering him, as if to reassure him that everything would be all right. He was among the hundreds of thousands of men whose time had come to register at the new government offices.

He sat in the living room chair for the last time. I sat adjacent to him in my spot. We didn't speak. His eyes moved slowly from the living room to my mother to me, as if he was trying to memorize every detail of what he was leaving behind.

CHAPTER 9

Puppy Love

I stood near the tree at the coffee stand with Thuy, bathed in the dull glow of the lantern. The rest of our group of friends were sitting, smoking cigarettes, and talking.

I tried not to look directly at Thuy, a girl the occupation had given me the courage to approach. She was a shy girl with a long veil of shiny hair and laughter that trilled like the vibrations of cicadas. Her closeness was both unnerving and exciting. I took in everything about her, the coolness of her skin and the thinness of her left earlobe. I felt the weight of her hair when she swept it from her shoulders, a gesture she often made to try and show she was confident in her beauty. She wasn't confident, though. Her shyness, her fragility, made her even prettier, more special to me.

"They are silly," Thuy said. She gestured toward the group where Chan was using wild arm gestures to tell a joke.

"Do you want to go back with them?" I asked.

"Not really." She laughed. I laughed too.

"Do you?" she asked.

"Not really," I said.

We laughed awkwardly.

Then we were silent. It wasn't quite raining, but there was a mist in the air.

It was strange to be out at night. The most subtle things had changed. The few of us who had gathered used softer voices. Every so often, the conversation stopped, and we glanced around furtively, making sure we weren't being watched. But the coffee stand was still ours.

I sneaked a glimpse at Thuy and saw her flinch then smooth her hair. Although she'd grown up wealthier than most of us, as a baker's daughter, she'd known work. The bakery was closed down. Girls went outside even less than boys. I wondered what she did to keep from getting bored.

I was conscious of Thuy's silhouette, though I didn't look up at her directly. She shifted from hip to hip. She flipped her hair.

I could barely breathe around her.

"Is everything okay, Thanh?" she asked.

"Fine. Why do you ask?"

"You seem quiet. Distracted."

"Yeah."

She waited, pulling her thin coat closed.

"Are you cold? You can wear my jacket," I said.

She shrugged shyly.

I tried to work up the courage to give her my coat. Instead, I stood there.

"Being here with you, it's normal."

She laughed. I joined her.

The words embarrassed me, but they were true. It was a miracle to me, hanging out with the other kids after everything that happened. Having Thuy as a girlfriend was a miracle. I'd never been able to talk to girls before.

"It's normal now," she emphasized.

I looked at Thuy, standing there with her arms folded across her chest.

"You are cold," I said. I took my jacket off and clumsily draped it over her shoulders.

CHAPTER 10

Goodbye

The absence of my father was felt a little less with each passing month. I focused on the toll that financial insecurity had taken on my mother. She would sit in the chair where my father once sat while telling his stories.

"I am going out," I said.

"Sit down, Thanh," she said.

I sat down. My mother's hands were folded in her lap. She'd assumed a certain air of authority, as was the case with women left behind in a city that no longer had any men. My mother was the one who slowly chipped at the gold bars we'd saved before authorities made us transfer the old bills to the new worthless ones they'd claimed equalized wealth. My mother would haggle over the price of dwindling supplies of rice and watercress in the market stalls when food was still available.

She had hopes for me. My escape was one of the last chances for our family.

"You must not tell anyone you are leaving," she said.

I nodded. I already knew this.

"Does the outfit fit you well?"

I smiled. Early the next morning, I would take a bus on a trip to a fishing village on the coast, disguised as an electrician. In my toolbox, I would carry my uncle's gun. I would hand the gun off to another guy.

"Yes, it fits. Do not worry, Mom."

"Of course, I am not worried. You are a capable boy."

Those were familiar words. They were the same words my parents used to describe my ability to score good grades after I'd proved myself by getting into the most prestigious high school in the city. My nature as a smart and obedient child fueled my parents' dreams for me to study abroad in the United States and to go to medical school. It was my mother's trust in me that made me the only son to know where the gold bars were hidden.

When they reopened high school, I was a shrewd student. I regurgitated the Communist propaganda integrated into our studies and passed the exit exams.

There was no motivation to pass, though. My family's military history ensured I'd never be allowed into college. Nothing made any sense.

My success relied on my escape. They'd send my older brother out, too, but in a different direction, knowing that it was likely only one of the boys would survive.

I thought my brother Thinh had a better chance of escaping successfully. He was street-smart. I was a studious boy who had never been outside of Saigon without my family. I had never even been in a fistfight. My confidence in my academic abilities was a lot stronger than my ability to wear disguises or to use a gun.

My mother glanced suspiciously around the room, as if the Communists were hiding.

"Tell me again the plan," my mother ordered.

"I will travel to the fishing village. We will meet the connection. We will stay overnight. Together, we will hijack a fishing boat and take it out to the ocean."

There was a small part of me that was excited for the journey. It was an adventure, the kind I had read about in the Chinese serialized stories by Jim Yong. At moments, it was easy to imagine myself as one of Yong's heroes, swooping in that sea town and battling my enemy, using my gun instead of martial arts and a magic sword. But in the clear daylight, I looked in the mirror at my protruding breastbone and frail arms and doubted I could do it. I secretly hoped I'd get word that the plan was intercepted before I even boarded the bus.

The plan was ludicrous. How was I going to hijack a boat? I imagined myself rocking in the dark murky water in the middle of the cold night. Everyone was trying to escape across the ocean to Malaysia, the Philippines, or Thailand, and hundreds were dying at sea.

One problem nagged at me. Despite my promise to my mother to keep our plans secret, I longed to share the news with Thuy. I thought she would be impressed with my heroism. And I didn't want to hurt her feelings by just disappearing.

That night, I traveled on my scooter in the pouring rain toward Thuy's house. Thuy was the only good thing about being stuck in Saigon. She understood me in a way nobody else did. I thought about the kind way she looked at me whenever I tried to explain something but couldn't. She always recognized the unsaid words.

When I got to the end of the street, I was so wet that the raincoat and my clothes clung to my skin. I stopped. I wanted to collect my thoughts and make myself look more presentable before intruding. I parked the bike and stood there.

Thuy was on the balcony with another boy. It didn't bother me. She had plenty of admirers. She charmed everyone. She was the wealthiest among our group of friends but didn't flaunt it. She was so pretty and shy that everyone wanted to protect her. But she was so private. Nobody could really reach her. That was the quality that made everyone treat her like a princess.

There was something about Thuy that really attracted me. There was a strength in her that made her more mature than the rest of us. It came out when she offered a rare line of insight or advice. Most often, she chose to remain silent. Maybe she didn't trust her wisdom in the defeated city in which we were living.

I stood under the tree like a madman. The rain was still dripping into my eyes and made them sting. I stared at Thuy in the dim light of the balcony. She was so beautiful, like a painting. I noticed, for the first time, the gentle way her pale chin tipped down in the light, at the way she kept her eyes toward the ground when she laughed. I knew that she liked me the best.

CHAPTER 11

Vung Tau

I sat on the bus in the early morning with my connection, the sun just beginning to cut through the sky. I looked sharp enough in my blue electricians outfit with my fake toolbox that nobody approached me. Besides, I'd kept my head down, biting my lip to keep from betraying my excitement. Occasionally, I looked up as the unfamiliar land rolled through the window.

Even though I had rice balls and dry shredded pork in my toolbox and was starving, I didn't eat at all during the four-hour ride.

When we arrived in Vung Tau, I was stunned. It was a tourist coastal town that I'd vaguely remembered going to with my family. The sun was shining, but it was deserted and gloomy. My mind raced as I played through the scenario my mother had drilled in my brain. At one point, I passed a police officer in his shiny uniform, but he barely glanced at me.

We sat by the empty house by the sea where we were supposed to meet our connection and sat near the front door. The longer we waited, the more my fascination intensified. The roughness of the sand tickled my palm. The cool brackish scent rolled off the murky sea. We lay there all day until the day ran out. Nobody came for me.

That night, I rode the bus home alone at night.

"Our only mistake was to trust the wrong people."

"Stop feeling sorry for yourself. You tried," my brother Thach said. My brother decided to try and cheer me up. "Do you want to go out for a coffee?"

Go away, go away, go away, I said to my brother in my head.

"There's no point. There's nothing to do," I whined, aware of how childish my voice sounded.

"Get over it. Stop moping," he said.

"I don't want to be here anymore. Saigon is so depressing. I wanted to get out."

"Everyone wants to get out of Saigon. You have to toughen up."

I didn't say anything but closed my eyes. I stayed that way until I heard my brother's footsteps as he left the room we shared.

CHAPTER 12

Sweet Blue Night

Thuy and I sat on her balcony in the dim light. The longer I had been back, the less comfortable I'd felt in Saigon. Being stuck at home every day was depressing. We had lost rights to our lives and our futures. There was nothing to do, nowhere to go. And I was getting tired of rotting in the house. Everything grated on my nerves. My younger brothers still screeched and annoyed me. My mother sat in my father's chair for hours, but she had stopped grieving for him.

Thuy and I sat on low stools. Her thin black hair hung down in a rope braid to the middle of her back. Her face had thinned out a little. She looked sadder.

"The funniest thing happened. On my way over here, I almost ran right into some of the soldiers doing their mock drills. They were all over the street, and I was just cruising by. It startled me, and I almost fell off the bike," I said.

"What happened?"

"Nothing. They probably saw me. But they just kept doing their weird drills, and I cruised on by."

I expected Thuy to laugh at this, but there was more gravity in her face. It was true my heart had dropped when it happened, but now it amused me. Every day I felt more invisible.

Things were getting worse. We occasionally heard about someone dragged out on the street and gunned down in front of everybody. A week previously, people were told to report anyone they believed to be involved in suspicious activities.

"You must be careful," she said.

"I know," I said, shuffling my feet on the balcony.

I looked past the outline of Thuy's delicate shoulder to a tree off the side of the balcony. As happened every time that I saw her, I regretted almost every word that I spoke.

"How are your studies going?" she asked politely.

I wanted to touch her shoulder. Thuy knew there was no way I was going to pass the college exams. I didn't really care about anything except finding a way to escape the country. The tests wouldn't help me get out.

"It is going okay," I said.

I still liked the way she looked at me.

"How is your mother?" I asked.

"Well, she's doing okay. Business is getting tough," she said.

She looked up at me, her black eyes pooled so deep it physically hurt me to see them. She never wanted to talk about her single mom and her relationship with another businessman. She was still herself, still self-possessed, but there was a sadness there, a desperation. I recognized it because I felt the same way myself.

And I couldn't handle it.

"What's wrong?" she asked.

"Nothing."

I thought about the other escape plan offered by my uncle-in-law. A group was going to take a train to the Central Highlands. They would cross through the jungle for weeks and then over a mountain pass before sneaking over the border into Laos. It was a dangerous plan. My mother encouraged me but said it was my choice to make.

I hadn't made the decision until that moment, sitting on the balcony with Thuy.

"I guess I just wanted to tell you it's been good, you know, spending time with you."

"Oh," she said, half a word and half a sigh.

Thuy was an intelligent girl.

"Do you understand?" I asked.

"I think so," she said. She nodded.

"It's not what I want. But there's no choice," I said.

She put up her finger as if to tell me to shut up.

Streetlights illuminated the empty district. It was impossible to tell who was left.

CHAPTER 13

Central Highland Jungles

I was bathed in a murky yellow lamppost light in Central Station. It made me tired. It was nearly midnight, the time when the train was supposed to arrive. The Reunification Rail would take us to the North, a line which ran from Saigon to Hanoi.

I'd never been in the train station at night before. It was an old station, built half a century previously by the French colonists. It was cold. I pulled my sleeves down to my wrists. The station was practically deserted.

The military backpack in which I'd stowed dry food and the rest of the khakis balanced heavily against my thigh. It was part of my disguise. Our group was posing as members of the Youth Corps. If I couldn't bribe the authorities to let me into college, this was one of the few legal options I had.

There were six of us standing in different parts of the station. The only one I knew was my uncle-in-law, who was near the door that led into the tracks. It comforted me to look around the station and see flashes of khaki. We communicated by secret hand signals.

I kept wishing the train would come. There was a policeman about a hundred feet away. I flinched when I saw him. I kept imagining he would target me because I was the youngest. I imagined him opening my pack and finding the escape tools, dried food, a machete.

"We will ride on the train for eight hours. Deep into the jungle."

I tried to imagine the jungle my uncle-in-law had described—the screeching monkeys, the poison snakes, bugs that broke the skin on your ankles to draw blood, the wet heat. There would be land-mines. There could be soldiers. We were supposed to walk for days, slicing the vines and plants with machetes, carefully rationing our water.

"All the way to the Central Highlands. We will stay overnight there at one of the small shacks. Then we cross the border at Laos."

I glanced at the other guys in khaki, all at least five years older, ex-soldiers with corded bodies and impenetrable stares. They didn't appear nervous like I was. They thought we could make the trip in less than a month. I trusted their confidence.

We left Central Station and plunged through a chain of poor neighborhoods. Each was the same. Makeshift houses with tin roofs were set close together on crooked streets.

The motion of the old rickety train was soothing, and I was exhausted. Every time my eyelids fluttered, I tried to force them open. I figured it would be safer to stay awake, even though the train would ride through the night. My alertness didn't last long. I drifted in and out of sleep, startling away every time we stopped at a station and people jumped on board.

Most of the passengers weren't permanent. They were vendors hawking goods or ticketless drifters. Kids hopped the train holding bundles of firewood, machetes on top of the pile. Women walked around with bags and boxes of dried goods like rice, sugar candies, and baby clothes. They drifted from compartment to compartment, trying to avoid the train conductor.

It didn't take too long before we had left the city behind. There was an open expanse of land.

I woke to see an official-looking man walking through the train car. I went to grab my electrician's box and my uncle's gun until I realized it wasn't there. It was the prop used for my previous escape attempt.

I looked through the window. Dawn had broken, but the land-scape was getting darker, deeper. Strange gnarled trees with thick vines blocked out the sky. Everything was a dark olive color, rotting. It had a nauseating scent.

This was a mistake, a voice echoed in my mind. *This place, it is death.*

Would I die in the jungle?

I guessed we were pretty far north. I recalled details of the route we'd be taking toward the Central Highlands that we had to cross. There would be a thin spot near the border where we would cross into Laos.

The guys we were escaping with were grown men. Most of them were military, with strong bodies and minds. They'd fought in jungles. They'd trained for this. I had never done anything that required more courage than taking the entrance exams or talking to Thuy.

At the same time, I didn't have a choice. There may not be another chance. There was nothing left in Saigon.

Toward the center of the train, I spotted a guy in khaki. He looked at me quickly and turned away. His arm was bent at the elbow over the armrest. He pointed two fingers toward the floor and split them.

I didn't remember what that signal meant.

A shadow passed over the train. We were crossing a mountain range that ran hundreds of miles. This was where the Ho Chi Minh Trail ran from the North to the South through Laos and Cambodia. The trail used by the Northern Army during the war and then occupied by the Khmer Rouge. I put my hand on my chest. The jungle trees were so dense and large, forming canopies of heavy dangling leaves that blocked out the sun. There was something about it that made me claustrophobic. We were so close to the border.

By late afternoon, I was no longer afraid. The right side of the train was completely ocean, in contrast to the dark arcane jungle. The coast offered an open beauty I had never seen before. Sun spilled down from the sky. Huge gray cliffs jutted over the wide blue waters as waves rolled and crashed. I glanced toward the left, where the dense green jungle blocked out the sky. That side was death. The blue ocean side was life.

I kicked my bag farther under the seat and walked over to the open door. I stood there, breathing in the salty air. It flooded my face, stuck to my teeth. The whole view was so beautiful.

The longer we traveled, the more I noticed. There were small fishing villages with shack houses painted in light colors, beaches with white-bone sand and small gentle waves. Others were rocky, waves violent. Some were so remote they seemed ancient, like nobody had visited them in a thousand years.

The longer I watched, the more power I witnessed. I had never seen my own country until that journey.

The makeshift hotel in the Central Highlands was adjacent to the bus station, at the end of a dirt road. It wasn't really a hotel but tiny and thatched cottages with tin roofs or hammocks strung on trees—a place where people could crash.

Compared to the hard benches on the train, the hammocks were luxury. It was funny to be in accommodations still surrounded by jungle and sky and sounds of crickets and hooting birds. I pulled the thin wool blanket up past my chest.

"The scouts have left. They will take a bus to the drop-off point to see what is going on," my uncle-in-law said. "Tomorrow morning, be ready early. We will wait for them to come back."

For a while, I lay awake, listening to the night sounds and feeling dread in my chest. I thought of the dense dark jungle we had passed. I thought of the crossing ahead and the hazards—poisonous snakes and plants, animal traps, soldiers, landmines, malaria. We had to be careful not to run out of water because dehydration could kill us. We had to run most of the time so we weren't spotted.

"Uncle?" I asked. I knew that he was still awake. "The other guys were all soldiers. Do you think we can make it?"

"Nephew, we will try."

CHAPTER 14

Oh, My Beautiful Country

I woke up before dawn and stood outside the lean-to, blowing smoke into the air. Everyone warned the Central Highlands were cold, but it wasn't a cold I was familiar with. I could feel it rattling my bones.

I pulled my green military coat over my sweater. The sun was beginning to stream through the clouds. The scouts weren't back yet. I hoisted my bag and walked to the restaurant near the hotel, which was just low bamboo chairs and shaky tables under a tin roof. The restaurant was attached to a small store.

"Welcome," a man said as I sat down. It was a special feeling to be the only one sitting down at a table in the Central Highlands jungle on the end of a dirt road. I ordered a coffee.

I looked down the dirt road into a thicket of trees. Frost hung off branches. Cloud light billowed over brown dirt.

The restaurant owner returned and put in front of me a sawed-off condensed milk can, half filled with steaming hot water. Then he poured some condensed milk into a coffee cup and put it into the can. He made some elaborate motions too quickly to follow.

The man fit a small coffee dripper and filter on top of the cup and packed the coffee in. He took the kettle and slowly poured steaming hot water over the dripper, expertly circling it around. He put the kettle back down on the stove and turned off the flame. He sat down on a chair while waiting for the coffee to steep.

Thin air slipped into my chest, snagging it. My fingertips felt strange and hard on the ends because they were so cold.

"Here you go," the waiter said, putting the whole contraption, including the sawed-off condensed milk can and a cup of fresh coffee, in front of me. He left. The scent of good strong coffee wafted up. That was something special in the Central Highlands.

I picked the cup up. My cold fingers were clumsy. I took a slow sip, letting the liquid trail down my throat. Then I took another. The coffee was amazing, the combination of good strong beans combined with the sweet hot of the condensed milk.

I sipped slowly, listening to the squawk of strange birds and trilling of insects. The sun was starting to rise low on the mountains.

The sun was high in the sky by the time the two scouts came back. I saw them at the restaurant, chatting with a man. I saw them signal to my uncle-in-law sitting at an adjacent table. But I couldn't make out their hands.

My heart was pounding. I kept remembering the jungle we saw from the train, and I looked through the window and noticed how dense the trees were, how they had swallowed up all the light. In the clear morning, I could finally see the mountains in the distance, huge looming beasts cutting out sky. Even if we managed to get through the jungle, we would have to cross those massive mountains.

It was a death trail.

How foolish I had been to volunteer for this escape plan!

I looked up and saw my uncle-in-law. He made a hand signal, fist clenched and thumb pointed down.

That signal meant no go. We weren't even going to try.

We took the late afternoon trains back, but we all split up to go to different places. We still had to be careful, but I felt bold enough to go to the car where my uncle was sitting. He gestured for me to sit down.

He was silent for a while, looking out the window. I waited. One plump lady walked through the aisles, selling cigarettes.

"There will be another opportunity," he said.

His voice was defeated. A part of me was relieved. Deep down, I didn't think I would make it. It would have been a death sentence.

"Yes," I said.

He was silent for a while, his lips tight. He kept touching his chin, like he was thinking about something important.

The train stopped. The woman with the cigarettes disappeared. It started again.

"What went wrong?" I asked.

He stopped touching his chin. He spoke low.

"The two scouts took a bus a few miles out, walked to the jungle border between Vietnam and Laos. There were checkpoints, trucks with soldiers. So they came back."

His voice had been strained when he spoke, as if it hurt him to confess the truth. He closed his eyes and soon was snoring, so I went back to my seat.

On the way back, the left side of the train was on the ocean side. I watched fishermen untangling nets, at an old woman carrying a basket on her head. I realized that I was happy because I was going to return to my city, my family and friends, and my girlfriend, Thuy.

Thuy. It felt like a lifetime ago I had met her, though it hadn't really been that long. I remembered the first time I knew I was special to her, when she let me put that jacket on her that night when we stood near the coffee shop. I remembered, too, the wise way she knew that I was going to leave without my having to say anything and the sadness that then passed between us.

I was going back to Saigon.

I was going to live.

At the same time, a part of me felt very ashamed of what happened. I didn't do anything wrong. But the second escape attempt had failed. Another opportunity might not occur.

Someone called out that we were approaching Tuy Hoa.

I looked out the window, excited. This was a famous town. There were folk songs written about it. Thinh had traveled there once and raved about Dai Lanh Beach.

Ngay xua toi da di ngang Tuy Hoa. Silently, I sang the tune in my mind.

I hurried over to the door. I did the trick where I could hang out of the train, feeling the sea air on my face, the wind whipping my hair. I was on the way back to my hometown, Saigon. It was the place where I belonged, for now.

When I arrived home, I tried not to look at my mother as I retold the story, the train ride through the dark jungle, the kids with the firewood and machetes, the French Vietnamese coffee in the tiny cold town. I looked only at my brother Thinh as I described the scouts who reached the border and determined we couldn't go farther.

"Nothing to do," he said as he nodded.

The younger kids were staring at me. My trip had made me more interesting to them since I had now been to places they hadn't known existed. I liked the way the kids were looking at me. I felt different too. I had been gone only a week, but I had aged years.

"There will be another chance. Maybe some other time," Thinh said.

"Yes," my mother responded in a thin voice.

I finally met her eyes. She looked disappointed.

It was strange to be back home after that trip. I was exhausted and depressed. I was sleeping during the day, as if I was still barreling on that train confused whether it was day or night. Once, I dreamed that I was still on the train, stranded out in the jungle. There were strange animals all around making shrieking noises. The strange light burned my eyes. The air was so heavy on my chest I could barely breathe.

CHAPTER 15

The Fateful Connection

My mother and I sat on a mat on the dirt, staring at the red sun lowering onto the brown dirt of an acre of land we had purchased. My two younger brothers, who were soaking wet from splashing in the ponds, were shimmying up a coconut tree.

Below them was a neat row of the spiky pineapple heads my family had planted.

"Will they grow, the pineapples?" I asked.

"Maybe. They will be sweet."

I smiled. It had only taken us an hour by bus from Saigon to get there. Ba Queo. It was so different, though. In Saigon, youth leaders patrolled the streets. If we were on the streets in the daytime, we needed a good excuse, or they would report us. It was a terrible feeling to realize every aspect of your life was scrutinized.

In our family's land in the country, we were unbothered. It was like a vacation. We went to the open-air market to buy food. Sometimes we ate at a restaurant.

We didn't really know what to do in the country, though. I'd watched my mother squatting in the dirt in her city clothes, picking at rocks with a small shovel while instructing my younger brothers where to plant the pineapple tops. I laughed.

"I thought it would be quieter out here," I said.

"It is quieter than Saigon."

"But there are so many noises. The birds and the frogs, the bugs."

My mother shooed away something buzzing in her face. We weren't used to spending so much time together. Parents in the city ran the household. They didn't care for their children. It wasn't our way. But our gold bars were dwindling. And most city maids and nannies had gone back to their families.

The land my mother purchased was so we'd have somewhere to go. When we traveled back to Saigon in the evenings, people would stare at us with our mud-streaked skin, bedraggled hair, and shiny tools. Our appearance suggested we'd taken Communist propaganda to heart. We were no longer lazy city people. We were industrious farmers.

I pointed out my brothers climbing the tree like monkeys, and my mother offered a rare smile. She no longer mourned my father. In a city without men, she'd adapted like everyone else. She found purpose trading what was left of our gold bars for rice in one of the few stores that still had food left. Or she organized escape routes for us boys.

Still, she always seemed tired, sad. I wondered if she had always been that way.

"They better not fall," she said.

She wiped the sweat from her forehead with a scarf and then handed it to me. It was still sticky out.

"It is arranged. You will deliver this envelope to Mr. Kha. They have arranged a connection to take you South. The Resistance. They will take you over the border into Cambodia, and then Thailand."

After weeks of coming out to the property and playing farmers, I'd almost forgotten why we were there.

"Good," I said.

I remembered the previous escape attempt, aborted. Of course, it hadn't been my fault. But I'd felt responsible for my mother's disappointment.

I couldn't stay in Saigon. I didn't want to be left behind with the girls.

"When?" I asked.

"Three days."

"Soon."

My brother jumped from the tree onto the dirt, landing with both his feet together. My mother watched for a while, distracted.

"He is a junkie too. The connection. Like Mr. Kha, they are rich."

"I understand."

"We will go back home and decide what to pack. You will take Thông with you."

I swallowed hard. I was surprised my mother had made this decision. Even before the war ended, it was understood that I would be the one to go abroad. But my older brother had been sent out, and all my attempts had failed. Thông was three years younger than me. The others were all too young.

My mother was sending her last two boys out to escape.

Kha's villa was in the center of Saigon, in the most affluent area I'd ever seen. Massive houses were separated by manicured gardens. Shocking green vines wound up the sides of trellises. A gardener was hosing water onto prickly vines.

The streets were empty. But it was a different feeling than the rest of the city where fear kept everyone inside. People preferred to stay indoors there, living in silence and decorum.

I stood in Kha's living room and rubbed the sudden goose bumps on my arms. Kha had an air conditioner that kept the rooms like the inside of an icebox.

The house had a funny smell, sweet like flowers at night, mixed with something heavy and resinous, like tree sap.

Kha had left me alone in the room. He'd kept it dark. In the far corner, there were high bookshelves and low cushions with pillows. On the table was a fine wooden box where he kept the long carved wooden pipes.

To me, this was just the way that wealthy people lived.

I wasn't naïve. In school, we'd learned all about the Opium Wars. Some kids knew people who visited dens. My father shared stories about American soldiers who got in trouble at the dens.

"Thanh, I have someone for you to meet," Kha said.

He was old and stooped. Still, his golden skin was practically unwrinkled and seemed to glow from the inside.

"This is Tám Điệu," he said.

A tall man walked up to me. He was at least sixty-five years old with dark eyeglasses. He had ruddy skin, flyaway hair, and was wearing an expensive jacket. But his white shirt was wrinkled, and his jacket wasn't buttoned correctly.

"Hello, Uncle," I said, bowing slightly.

Tám Điệu smiled. His teeth were stained brown, and a few were broken.

"So this is the young man who will go on a journey with me."

"With my brother also, sir."

He looked me over. Everything about him seemed comical, especially his squished-up eyes.

"Ah, nice young man like you. I am sure you are breaking the young girls' hearts when you leave," he said. Then he laughed.

I couldn't think of any way to respond.

My silence made him laugh harder. He took a step closer and breathed in my face. His mouth had a weird smell, like burnt paper.

"Okay, we leave in two days. Meet me at the Luc Tinh bus station."

Tám Điệu had a slow cloying confidence. There was something mesmerizing about him, like the flame of a candle. I just stood there, staring.

"Go now. Prepare," he said.

CHAPTER 16

Southern Land

My brother Thông and I sat on the bed in the hotel room in Long Xuyen. We had at least eight hours before it was dark enough to travel. We were both restless, fidgety. Thông kept getting up and sitting back down on the blue plastic chair that was in the corner of the room. I was propped up on the bed with the pillow behind my back and with my hands crossed behind my head. The television was on with no sound. We wanted to stay low.

"I wish that we could go home," Thông said.

"You mean home to your real parents in the jungle tribe?"

Thông didn't laugh like I'd hoped.

"Relax, brother. This is an adventure," I said.

"Some adventure. We are stuck in this room."

I walked to the window and peeked past the curtains. There was just a tiny empty street. I remembered how my father combatted boredom for weeks before he turned himself in.

"Hey, Thông. Do you remember when Dad rented out our house to the American GIs from Tan Son Nhut Air Force Base, so we were living in Uncle's garage?"

"That metal garage? It was so hot."

The whole place was made of aluminum, so hot in the daytime we stripped down to our underclothes to do homework and so cold at night that we had to huddle for warmth to sleep.

"It was tough for me to explain to you younger kids why we were living there. Why did we? Because he found some American GIs from Tan Son Nhut Air Base to rent the entire house to. And when the war was going on, only way anyone made any money at all was by catering to the American soldiers. The hotels were able to stay in business. Everyone else suffered, but Dad knew how to make money from very little."

My brother started messing with the television channels. I lay down on the bed and tried to remember that time.

If the Communists were really smart or knew what they were looking for, they would have known Russ was staying at our house because of the screen door. Russ was the only one left out of four and stayed in just one room. It was one of our father's concessions to him, like the maid who made his bed and cooked him eggs and bacon. Russ wasn't used to sleeping under mosquito nets like we were, so we got him the screen door. All the houses that were rented to the American soldiers had screen doors.

The screen door didn't work perfectly, of course. Although some of their tiny insect carcasses were stuck to the screen, many squirmed past it and into the house. My official afternoon job was to walk around the house with my dad, snapping my favorite red towel in the air to shoo the mosquitoes away. I was waving it enthusiastically because it was my Thursday to get takeout Chinese food.

Our family liked Chinese wonton noodles, a taste passed down from my grandpa, who was wealthy enough to eat at fancy restaurants in Vietnam's Chinatown. It was one of the few luxury items my father allowed us. When my father learned that Russ liked Chinese wonton noodles too, he incorporated him into our Thursday tradition. My father was closer to Russ than to other American soldiers, and he tried to make his life as luxurious as possible.

Out of eight, only four of my brothers and sister were around. I was old enough to ride on the back of my dad's motorbike and hold the takeout food.

"It's Chinese Food Day. It's my turn, Dad."

I arrived with my father at the restaurant. The street was like a carnival. Red lanterns glowed in between a row of streetlamps. Women wearing silk dresses walked alongside dark-suited men. Steam rose from street vendor carts.

My father and I both walked inside quickly, our mouths and bellies hungry for the wonton noodles, thick steamy broth, sweet jellied desert.

It was like being transported to another world.

"Don't forget, we will need one bowl for takeout," he said.

Even in those years, before any of us really knew hunger, there was something about that rich soup that was sacred. I knew it every time I stared at the steam lifting off the clear liquid, when I slowly raised it to my mouth, slurping it and making the sucking sound that told everyone how much I enjoyed it. I could see it in my father's veiled eyes, how he picked up the bowl with both hands, tilting it toward his raised head.

After the busboy took our plates away, the waiter came with two bowls of sweet black tapioca jellies. We leaned back. My stomach was round and hard and full. Then he came back with Russ's tiered silver takeout container, the bottom container with scorching hot broth, the middle one with the noodles and meat and vegetables, the third with the wontons.

My father nodded at me. It was my responsibility to hold Russ's food while riding on the back of my father's Lambretta. I would grip my father's back with one hand and the container with the other. It was a sweet torture. I was a small boy wearing shorts, and I struggled to prevent the food from spilling onto my naked thigh and burning me.

Only in the darkness could we breathe. My brother and I slipped down the street. I tried to walk languidly while my brother was practically skipping. The fresh air felt so good on our faces. We walked silently through the strange city over the canals and crooked streets, almost as if we didn't exist.

"I want to eat some shrimp stew over rice," my brother said.

"Okay. If they are there," I said.

In my pocket, I had money. My mother had traded some of her gold. In the past, I'd never had my own money. I usually ate the meals my mother organized. I'd never once ordered my own meals from street vendors or restaurants.

I looked down the street at rows of old red tile roof houses, men sitting on stools on the gaslit porches.

"Remember the Chinese food we used to get for Russ?" I asked.

"I don't know. No," he said.

My brother seemed to be better at forgetting than I was. He'd always been an awkward kid. He didn't excel at school. He didn't have many close friends. Maybe it was easier for him to be placeless than me because he'd never been where his path had been decided for him.

By this time, we knew the bends of the streets in the city, leading us to the river where the street vendor sold us food. Our small table was set up.

"Hello," I said when we got to the vendor.

"Two," he said, greeting us in his funny Southern accent. He smiled as he started spooning food into bowls for us. I was sure the man knew we didn't belong in that small city, that we were on the run. But Tám Điệu had introduced us when we'd first arrived. And the vendor seemed trustworthy. He'd likely seen many people passing through on the way to the border.

We took our food and sat down at the little table. We were the only ones. We couldn't hear the river, but we knew it was sloshing beside us. In the wind, there was the sound of someone playing a reedy instrument.

"It's nice here," my brother said.

"Don't get too comfortable, though."

"If I have to stay another night in that hotel, I may turn crazy."

I smiled. In the distance, we could hear a strange insect with a chirping sound and something like a frog. I watched the vendor wiping oil from the cooking dish as my brother slurped up his stew.

"He is coming tomorrow. Tomorrow is the third day," I said.

My brother nodded, forcing the food in his mouth.

"Slow down. You are going to get a stomachache."

My brother smiled and then spit out some food and laughed.

I started to scold him but began laughing myself. Everything about our situation was hilarious. For some reason, it felt even crazier than my previous escape attempts. And hanging out with Tám Điệu had given a festive air to everything. He made us laugh so often, we forgot to be scared. He was coming the next day.

CHAPTER 17

Wandering

My brother and I walked a few paces behind Tám Điệu as usual. It was a kind of slum we were traveling through. Trash had piled in an alley next to an empty hotel. Wood was nailed over the window of a rickety store. Animals wallowed in the mud near thatched-roof houses.

This countryside was the exact opposite to Mr. Kha's luxurious neighborhood where the houses were set wide apart, and gardeners, maids, and street sweepers worked. They were both quiet places, but this one felt dangerous. Behind broken windows and empty stalls, I felt that everyone was watching us.

"Dirty place," my brother whispered.

"Be quiet," I said.

He looked at me. His eyes sparkled. From the moment we'd arrived in the South, it had felt like a magical adventure. Everything about it was so different from life in the city—the strange accents, sweet low bellowing chords from a musical instrument I wasn't familiar with, the disorienting walks following the maze of canals.

"Everyone's looking at us," he said.

"Slow," I said.

I let my eyes drift from Tám Điệu's back to the few people on the steps of the row of houses we were approaching. Girls sitting on the steps were wearing high heels and Western shirts that showed off their shoulders and stomachs. They eyed us suspiciously.

"Hello, beauties. Is Lieu around?" Tám Điệu said.

One of the girls bent toward Tám Điệu's face with her low-cut top, as if making a joke with her chest. The other switched from one hip to another then tossed her long dark hair.

Tám Điệu whispered something to them. The girls both laughed.

My brother started cracking up for no reason. Tám Điệu's charms were amazing. Everywhere we went, people responded to it.

With him, we would always be safe.

The sun was low, bleeding pink on the horizon of the rice paddy as we walked up the long dirt road. It was empty except for a frog screeching. I imagined the fetid water in the dark canals and terrifying animals waiting for us to come closer. Bats circled the tops of coconut trees.

"We are almost there. You boys will wait in the courtyard."

"Yes, Uncle," we both answered.

I slapped a mosquito off my neck. It made me more aware of how many were feasting on my body, on the inside of my thighs and my ankles. My brother skipped beside Tám Điệu. It occurred to me that I was thirsty, and we had not had anything to eat since breakfast.

The brick ranch house had a yard that was larger than I'd ever seen. It was the house of a rich country person. We sat on a stone table in the courtyard while Tám Điệu knocked on the giant door and disappeared inside.

"It will get cold, brother," Thông said.

I nodded. The sky was turning from blue to black.

"It smells here, like bad eggs," my brother added.

"It is just the land breaking down, the way plants break down in water."

"Phew…"

"Be quiet. Behave."

Thông obeyed me. It was strange for me to command the responsibilities of the elder brother, but it was important to keep him safe.

"Look through the window," Thông said.

We both watched an old man carry an oil lamp to a table where our uncle was sitting. Behind them, there was a girl around my age. She was wearing black clothes like pajamas and carrying a tea tray.

"How long will we stay here?" Thông grumbled.

"We stay until he does what he needs to inside."

"That's not what I mean," my brother said.

The girl leaned over in the lamplight, and I could see pale skin. There was a sweetness to the way she smiled at them. Then she gently bowed her head.

She reminded me of Thuy, somehow.

Something occurred to me. My brother and I were on the run between worlds. We weren't able to do anything normal anymore, like be outside or make friends. It was the first time that reality hit me.

"I mean," Thông continued, "how long will we stay with Tám Điệu? How long will we stay in the villa?"

I was reminded of our mission there: to meet up with the resistance, to find a way out of the country, a place where we would be safe.

"Until it is time," I said, echoing Tám Điệu's words earlier that day.

I looked at the house. The two men were chatting. The girl was no longer there.

CHAPTER 18

Strange Friends

We were in the beautiful French brick villa in Long Xuyen where Tám Điệu sometimes left us. The house was at the foot of a long concrete bridge. I liked to stand there and watch the sun getting lower and purple-red light spread over the bridge and across the wide river.

In this house, we stayed on the top floor. We were rarely allowed outside. Tám Điệu left us there when he went on longer trips back to Saigon. Tám Điệu was a mysterious man. He came and went all the time. Sometimes we tried to figure out what Tám Điệu's job was. He was always very busy arranging something that took a lot of figuring and coordination. We guessed he was helping other people too.

We trusted he would always come back for us.

And he always did.

I stood against the wall in our bedroom when I heard footsteps coming up the stairs. I sat on the bed. My brother pretended to play with a deck of cards.

Mr. Vinh entered the room. He was taking care of us for Tám Điệu. Mr. Vinh and Tám Điệu had been friends ever since they were children. He was a retired lawyer who wore clean suits. He didn't like the Communists.

"Are you boys doing okay?" Mr. Vinh asked in his soft-spoken manner.

Mr. Vinh had a kind wife and a daughter who was a teacher. The family seemed normal compared to Tám Điệu. I wondered if he knew about what Tám Điệu did. I didn't think he would have approved.

"We are fine, Uncle. Thank you for asking us."

"You boys must get so bored up here. Well, anyhow, Tám Điệu is downstairs. He wants you to get ready."

My brother's face broke out in a big smile. It had been a long time to be trapped inside.

* * *

We sat on a bench at the edge of the city, drinking tea. Tám Điệu was excited, the mood of his I liked best. He was never mean to us, but he could be distant, which made me uncomfortable.

In front of us was a vendor, ladling something hot into cups. Next to him, a farmer was roasting something in a metal barrel. It smelled unfamiliar but good. Two women walked by, talking loudly in their strange Southern accent.

"The chickens keep squawking," Tám Điệu said.

Thông giggled, covering his hand with his mouth like a young boy and not fifteen years old.

"Their poor husbands will lose their hearing soon, all those chickens pecking at them," Tám Điệu said and laughed.

"When this is over and someday you marry your girl, be careful. Don't let her tongue sting you, nephew," he said and punched me lightly on the shoulder.

But Thuy isn't like that. She's a sweet girl, I thought.

"We are going to see some important people tonight. Just listen but don't talk. You learn more that way. Right, Thanh?" Tám Điệu continued.

"Right, Uncle."

CHAPTER 19

It Is Time to Go

The meeting spot was in a town along the highway at the intersection of Vietnam and Cambodia. As we and Tám Điệu got off a small bus, a column of tanks passed us, traveling outward toward the border. This was the site of multiple months of battles with the Khmer Rouge.

It was April 30, 1977, exactly two years after the fall of Saigon, when I had stood on that hospital roof and watched the city exploding beneath me.

Tám Điệu hurried my brother toward an open-air market. It was a strange empty land with long fields and thatch-roofed houses where the occasional farm animal stood.

We weren't used to being outside the hotel room.

It was strange to see people going about their daily lives after all those weeks of hiding out in that bleak hotel. It was too much to take in the loudness of the people yelling in funny accents as they bargained for food and clothing. Even the scent of the market was unnerving, a bitter smell of vegetables and something fecund and sweaty, like farm animals.

We were finally going to meet one of Tám Điệu's friends, a member of the resistance who was going to smuggle us across the border from Cambodia and then into Thailand. After all those months of false starts, of tagging along on Tám Điệu's mysterious trips, of being shuttled from the hotel to Long Xuyen or back to Saigon, we were finally making our escape. We'd said goodbye to my mom and our friends so many times that nobody believed we would actually leave.

My brother's dark skin made him look more like the people in the South where we stood than anybody in our family in Saigon. I wondered if this would protect him where we were headed.

Thông was distracted by the magic of the market. I was nervous we would get caught.

Please let this work out okay, I prayed, reminding myself my job was to protect him.

Tám Điệu stopped us abruptly. We stood facing a man. He was kind of short and bulky. He squeezed my shoulders.

"Thanh, Thông, this is Hai. He is going to take care of you from here. He will take you to the next meeting spot. You do what he says, okay?"

Tám Điệu looked at me with trust, knowing I was mature enough to do what had to be done. And suddenly, he turned around, and I watched his back.

Hai was a large man. There was something about the way his eyes narrowed as he looked at us that felt strange.

"Follow me," he said. We had to run to follow him through the open market, tunneling through screaming crowds. I kept my brother in front of me so I could see him.

It was late afternoon, and the sun was low on the horizon. The market was filled with people doing their grocery shopping. We hadn't eaten much that morning, and I was dizzy.

Tám Điệu had told us there were other people in the market waiting to be picked up and delivered to the next spot.

"Okay, wait here, and then they will come pick you up," Hai said.

He barely looked at us. His large body wound through the crowds and disappeared.

I don't know how long we stood there, waiting. I was watching a woman choosing plums from a market stall, squeezing each one. She was wearing the simple clothes of the villagers, a plain white blouse and black pants. A vendor was standing behind the table, impatient.

"Thanh!" I heard my brother scream.

I saw a group of men rolling up in their jeeps then getting out and running toward us. There were at least ten of them, men in official dress, khaki green military and yellow of the police, with rifles and sticks in their hands. It didn't occur to me that we were in danger. I was focused on the rhythmic way they ran, as if they were one body.

They descended on us, screaming, guns pointed at our faces.

The people in the market were going about their regular business. Surely somebody would help us. But we didn't know anyone there.

"Leave us alone. We didn't do anything!" I yelled.

They started to grab us roughly. One slapped my shoulder hard.

"We didn't do anything. Please!" I yelled.

My heart thudded loudly in my ears.

"Be quiet or we will shoot you right on the spot!" one snarled.

I swallowed.

There was a buzzing hive-like sound all around me.

Everything was so far away.

They pulled our hands behind our backs. Pain shot through my back, and I realized they were using rope to tie us up. My brother was crying.

"It's okay, Thông," I tried to say, but no words were coming out of my mouth.

One of the men slapped me.

People had gathered around us. They all looked so sorry for us.

The men kicked and pushed us and started to lead us away.

We sat in the small open van. There were about ten other guys.

Thông's lip was split, and he kept trying to shift his body so the ropes wouldn't hurt him. There were tearstains on his cheeks, but it was his expression that haunted me. I had never seen my brother so scared.

It was my fault. I was supposed to protect him.

"Don't worry. They will come for us," I told him.

As the vans started rolling, I imagined that Hai or Tám Điệu would save us. I imagined the resistance stopping the van, shooting everyone and rescuing us.

The van bumped along the road. The air from the road was sticky on my cheeks. As we moved toward the town, another column of tanks was moving in the other direction toward the border.

CHAPTER 20

Chau Phu District Jail

The guard stretched out the barbed wire on a wooden door and pushed his flashlight into our cell—a brick room converted from a former army barracks. His flashlight bobbed across the closed eyes, illuminating all the sleeping men.

There were two rows of twelve of us, our feet facing each other, our heads pressed against adjacent walls. Each row of men was pressed shoulder to shoulder. Our ankles were shackled, the shackles attached by a long metal pole fixed to the wall.

"Who's guarding now?" the guard whispered. The whisper was deliberate. They tried to determine if the man on assigned shift was asleep so they could punish him the next day.

I pushed myself up to a seated position, careful not to jerk the metal pole.

"Thanh!" I screamed out, my voice ragged.

The ghost remained silent. The flashlight bobbed. Eventually, he moved on.

The stale air was cool enough to sleep in but not enough to take away the stench of diarrhea and the odor of open sores on legs and butts from being in the same position on the dirt floor for months.

To my left was a man who'd earned the rare privilege of having one ankle shackle removed. He could lay on his side. His breath was hot on my neck. I was so jealous of his mobility.

I listened to my brother Thông's light snores on my right. I was glad he was resting. For a few hours at least. For a few hours, he was relieved of the sting and itch of the boils on his butt and thighs, a result of sweating on the dirty mattress for so long.

It hurt my heart to know my brother was suffering. My mother had trusted me to protect him. I had let her down. But I didn't know what I'd done wrong.

I replayed our last hours in the market. We'd been standing exactly where Hai had told us to stand when the cops and military shoulders surrounded us, yelling and shoving us until they had tied us and thrown him on the van. It had all happened so quickly.

I remembered my brother's face while we were in the van.

Don't worry. They will come for us, I had told him.

But they hadn't come back for us. Perhaps we weren't important enough.

My brother moaned.

I pressed my shoulder closer to him, just to let him know I was there.

* * *

There were three types of people jailed along with us. Most were farmers and peasants from the South. A few had been arrested for ordinary crimes, like beating their wives, street fighting, visiting prostitutes, and being thieves.

There were more that were Nationalists that believed in independence from both the French and the Communists, most of them part of the Hoa Hao religion which dominated the Mekong Delta. Hoa Hao is an offshoot of Buddhism that catered to the poorer people. Their founder, Huynh Phu So, made Buddhism more accessible. It was based on simple poetic teachings, had few temples and statues, and did not require priests or lofty contributions. They believed that Huynh Phu So was disappeared by the Communists in 1947 and that their prophet would return as the Buddhist in the future. They were among resistance forces that refused to surrender in 1975 after the Communists took over.

Although we didn't receive any formal charges, other guys were in jail either because they tried to flee the country or were part of the resistance. The guys Tám Điệu was trying to connect us with were followers of Hoa Hao.

The guys in the jail were kind to one another. They were idealists who possessed the calmness that may have come from their religious belief in a better life after death or from having livelihoods dependent on moon tides and the amount of sun or rain that came. I never heard anyone raise their voices in anger. They showed their compassion in small gestures, like the way they treated the old man with one arm with respect because he was their elder.

I trusted they would take care of us too.

"Don't force him, nephew," the old man said to me. I had been holding the bowl to my brother's chin, pinching rice on his chopsticks. He kept moaning and pushing his head toward the wall.

"The diarrhea is still bad. I have more medicine," he said.

The old man with one arm was looking out for my brother. When we were well, he'd given us both a rare treat—sugar cubes one of his visitors must have brought. There was no shortage of food even in the jail. Rice and vegetables were abundant, but there were no sweets.

I watched the old man pass a small ladle-like spoon down the row until it finally got to me. I smelled it. It was a paste he'd made from plants he ground up with a rock and added water to. It tasted awful, but it worked. I didn't know why it wasn't working on my brother.

I touched my brother's shoulder lightly.

"This is medicine. Drink it."

My brother moaned.

"Lift your head. It will make your stomach better. Swallow it. It's a gift."

My brother did as I said but started gagging. I wiped whatever had come off his chin. He put his head back down.

I returned to my own bowl. I liked to eat in small doses. My stomach had shrunken. I had watched how other guys learned to ration small pleasures.

I dug into my bowl with my chopsticks and found rice and pickled vegetables. Next to it was a small morsel of meat. I found it disgusting when we first came to the jail. It was chuột đồng, a big chubby rice paddy rat, skinned and roasted on spits. I'd gotten used to it. Still, as I picked it up in the sticks and started eating it, I was aware that the spongy consistency could give way to the crackle of bone.

"Nguyen Tuong Thanh!" a guard bellowed from outside the door. My stomach dropped. I closed my eyes briefly. I didn't know how much longer I could keep it up.

The old man sighed. I looked toward him. He was sitting near the wall with his thirty-five-year-old son, their heads bent toward each other as if communicating telepathically.

The guards banged the metal locks and swung open the door.

"Be strong, nephew. We will look after your brother," the old man whispered.

I stood up, bracing my watery knees, and made my way toward the door.

CHAPTER 21

Interrogation

I sat in a chair with my wrists and ankles tied. I hadn't yet gotten used to sleeping on my back with my ankles tied, so I hadn't slept in days. At the same time, the dirty room had made me disoriented. They hadn't given us any water, and my throat was so dry, as if I had no saliva in my mouth.

Mr. Nam, nickname Nam Tham, the jail warden, was still yelling at me. He was a chubby and cruel man, at least fifty. His voice was sharp and his eyes beady.

"Speak to me!" he boomed. "Answer me."

"I already told you. I don't understand what you are asking."

He walked up to me again, his fat cheeks pulsing. He slapped me so hard across the mouth that I could feel the bones of his hand on my jaw. My bladder loosened.

It was my fourth time in the room but the first time he had hit me. I knew that some guys had been tortured.

He sat down in his chair in his fancy shoes. Slowly, he crossed his ankle over his knee. He was silent.

I was so tired. I just wanted to sleep.

"Thanh. Nephew. I know you are a good boy. This would be a lot easier for you if you just told me what I needed to know. Then you can go back to the cell with your brother and rest. Would you like that?"

I looked up but knew better than to meet his eyes.

"I told you. I don't know who they were."

"How did you get to the market?"

"I took a bus from Saigon."

"Who told you to go to the market?"

"I don't know. My mother arranged it. She just told me what bus to get on."

"Just tell me the truth. Then this goes away. What did you and your brother do for the resistance?"

I thought back to all those nights in the hotel room in Long Xuyen. All the errands we went on with Tám Điệu. The prostitutes in the alley. The trip we made to the countryside. The beautiful girl who served tea.

"My brother is only fourteen. He is innocent. He didn't know a thing. Please let him go."

I'd known what my father and uncle believed, fighting in the Southern Army. But since that night on the hospital roof, I couldn't even grasp what had happened to my country. I fled because I was supposed to, but that was neither rebellion nor cowardice.

"What is his name?"

"I don't know."

"You know. What is his name?"

He stood up again and walked over. He slammed his hand on the metal table next to me. I jumped. He smiled and moved closer.

"You are lying," he whispered, his breath on my cheek.

"I'm not lying. I don't know who they are, please," I said as he paced back to the chair.

"How did you get to the market? Who set it up?"

I couldn't remember what I had told him already. I wouldn't tell them that I met with Tám Điệu. I wasn't going to be the person who gave them the resistance.

"I didn't meet anyone. I didn't even know who I was going to meet. Just some people. They were going to get us across the border."

I heard a *click, click, click*. The warden was moving his big finger across a Zippo lighter, watching as the flame rose. I watched his pudgy thumb and saw the flame rise. *Click, click, click.*

"Don't lie to me!" he yelled. He threw the lighter, and I felt it graze my cheek before it smashed against the wall.

* * *

We stood in a single file in the courtyard as it filled with sunlight. Beyond the barbed wire was a long country road and a few houses engulfed by a rice paddy. Farther down was a small open-air market where the cooks bought our food. There was a canal beyond the market where our water was hauled. The road eventually led to Chau Doc, a large town on the border of Cambodia, about fifteen miles away. We sometimes heard the explosions from heavy fighting going on there.

"Okay," the guard in the front of the line said gently. We called him Brother Six because his parents had named him Six, as he was the fifth born in his family. It was a tradition in the Mekong Delta to count kids on the second number.

Brother Six, in his late twenties, made an extra effort to be kind. The other guards respected him because he was older and even keeled. The way he treated us made it obvious he wasn't a Communist but became a police officer only to make a living.

"Maybe they will put us back on the bus," Quoc whispered, tapping me on the shoulder. He started laughing.

Quoc slept next to me and my brother, and we had become good friends. He was from Saigon, too, and had been in college when the war ended.

"Yeah. This time they will take you to the border," I said.

"Or to Thailand," he said giddily. "Most expensive bus ticket you can think of."

That was the joke he always told when he talked about how he wound up at Chau Phu District Jail. He was one of the guys who had paid someone who promised the resistance would take him to Cambodia. Instead, they took a few buses, and instead of taking them to a meeting spot, the last bus took them straight to jail.

"Ten more guys came in yesterday. They were tricked too," he whispered.

"Quiet!" one of the guards yelled. We shut up.

The daylight stung our eyes. My knees felt weak as we walked through the field toward the end of the road. We passed the district office where they had taken me for the interrogations. I tried not to look up. The interrogations had stopped a week before, suddenly, but my mind and body were still exhausted from them, my eyes so sticky they didn't want to open. The last session had been two weeks before. For some reason, they had just stopped.

I wanted to believe they had given up. But I knew better than to hope.

It felt so good to be outside. With each step, the circulation returned to my legs. The humidity in the morning air felt nice on the back of my neck. The sickness had finally passed from my bowels. Other guys were not as lucky.

My brother was stumbling in front of me, and I willed him not to fall. Sometimes I squeezed his shoulder, offering reassurance.

"So pretty," Quoc said when we got to the pond.

"Smells good," my brother joked back.

The pond was oval-shaped and fifty feet long. It was greenish. But when you looked closely, you could see a thick layer of scum on top and brown chunks floating around. It was human waste. Above the pond was a toilet seat where we relieved ourselves every morning.

Some guys were standing at the gasoline drum. It was filled with canal water, and we used it to brush our teeth and wash our faces.

The area was designated to farm the basa fish. They were part of our diet. They put the toilet there deliberately, and the basa fish got plump on human waste.

CHAPTER 22

Another Brother

After dinner, the guards put back the shackles on our legs for the night. We were still too sick to do much. We lay there and talked. Behind our wall was another room where we could hear other prisoners speaking faintly. Their murmurs were comforting. Our oil lamp burned. The fumes stunk.

I drifted in and out of consciousness, every so often remembering Thuy's sweet face on the balcony that night I watched her from that street in the rain, imagining sitting on that balcony after I was freed, her compassionate face while she listened to the story about what I had been through.

A commotion snapped me out of it. There were brutal sounds of guards yelling mixed with the hollow sound of somebody being punched, ending with metal thwacking against rock. A door slammed. The voices rose and then fell.

Our room captain went to the wall to find out what happened. Another voice informed him that they had someone from Saigon, newly captured. Then I heard a familiar voice on the other side of the wall.

"Thanh, are you there?"

"Oh my god, Thach! What are you doing here?"

"Mother sent me to look for you. And they arrested me too."

My younger brother heard Thach and started crying hysterically, perhaps because all three brothers were now locked up. Who would save us now?

A few days later

I sat on the floor. My body surged with adrenaline, the way it could get after I'd gone to the toilet but before being chained up again. My legs cramped. My excitement was overwhelming when I couldn't walk it off.

Thông was playing Chinese chess with the old man. I saw Thông's childlike excitement while he moved the pieces on the board. Thông had always been a confident child. Now he was beginning to doubt his ability to do things, even things as simple as games.

Thông was the opposite of most of the older guys in our room who seemed to train themselves to go numb. His emotions were explosive. I was relieved when they stopped interrogating us because I feared that Thông would talk about Tám Điệu and get us in trouble.

I looked around. Some guys were writing in notebooks, others having conversations. Some lay still with glossy eyelids and inert bodies, like caterpillars in the cocoon.

"I have news, Thông," I said quietly.

Some guys pretending to sleep shifted to eavesdrop.

"What?" he said in a singsong voice, like he was barely paying attention to me. He jumped the wooden piece a few times on the board. "Good news or bad news?" he asked.

"Certainly good news."

He looked up from the board then.

"Thach…he's been released."

It took a few seconds for this to sink in.

"Oh," Thông said and went back to studying the board.

"It's good news," I repeated.

"Wonderful. He is free," the old man said, nudging Thông.

"But why, Thanh? Why did they let him go?"

"They realized he didn't have any information. He didn't have anything to do with the resistance," I said.

He nodded then returned to studying the board.

I suddenly guessed what my brother was thinking: *Why him? Why not us? We don't know anything either.*

Thông jumped a few chess moves and laughed at the old guy who he had just outsmarted.

CHAPTER 23

The Unexpected Storyteller

We lay on our backs with our legs cuffed in the dark, visible in the glow of the oil lamp. I had the room listening to me as I recited from memory my Chinese serial stories. I took a deep breath between lines, making sure to make my voice strong enough to reach everyone. The men and women in the surrounding rooms, who usually sang their country songs after dinner, were absolutely silent. I felt everyone in my room, my friends and my brother, hanging on my every word.

I couldn't believe what was happening. There was a power in the stories themselves. After I started to tell them, I didn't feel shy.

"Well, Tiêu Thập Nhất Lang is the hero, a great fighter. But there was also a female knight named Phong Tu Nuong, very beautiful but also very brave. She could fight like a man. She did swordplay, and she could slip through the air undetected and surprise her enemies."

I glanced outside the barbed wire window. Flashlights bobbed through blackness. I made out at least three bodies. One of them was the chief of police. He came in at night for his shift after fat Mr. Nam left for the day. Even he was listening to me.

There was a gravity to the fact that important people were listening to me. The attitudes of the police chief and guards seemed to be subtly changing with each story I told. They weren't angry anymore. The stories pacified them somehow.

I was more humbled by the attention of the guys in the rooms, with their sinewy muscular bodies and their cracked hands. These were brave guys with deep beliefs they had sacrificed their freedom for, beliefs for which they were willing to lose their lives. They had a calmness toward the guards' anger and the harsh conditions that made them lifetimes older. They may not have gone to college, but they were more sophisticated than us boys from Saigon.

As I spoke, a part of me entered the stories. I was transported back to my bedroom in Saigon, where I lay on my cushy bed with my ear cupping a real pillow, reading the forbidden magazines. I remembered the dim afternoon sunlight through the shuttered window, the din of noise in the narrow street, the way the torture of those long dull afternoons was alleviated as I got lost in the story. The lack of a purpose, the absence of a future, had given me permission to dream.

I'd never before truly believed it was possible for warriors to fly through the air. And I could feel the pull of the history of the stories that stretched back thousands of years, the martial arts and ancient Taoist philosophy, the balance of energy. My reality was transcendental, not limited to the discomfort of my stiff back and slack muscles, my concave rib cage or chafed ankles.

Although these stories from famous writers in Singapore and Hong Kong were reprinted in newspapers around the world and had millions of readers, they were completely foreign to the guys in the jail. Still, they were enraptured the same way those readers were, who had to read the stories chapter by chapter when they were printed in the paper, for twenty or thirty weeks before they had finished a whole novel.

Of course, I hadn't memorized every detail of the story or the exact order. I remembered sitting on my clean bed in my clean clothes with the rental book in my hands, the soft worn feel of the pages the way the words looked.

I remembered my father sitting on the chair on those final days telling stories.

Of course, I hadn't memorized every detail of the story or the exact order. But nobody noticed. I made the rest up.

"It was the most beautiful land you could ever imagine. It was hilly, not flat like here. And it was so lush. There were green grasses and purple wildflowers and birds with long thin beaks that sucked the juice out of them and made the air heady with their song. You could smell the flowers everywhere. It was the most beautiful trilling sound, and there were rivers that wound through the hills with the purest water that everybody could drink." The vibrations of my voice and the pretty language and imaginary valley where the saga took place energized me. I was in awe of my newfound confidence to tell the stories, to bring a magical world that might have existed parallel to our own to a bunch of guys locked in a room they might never be allowed to leave.

A few nights later, we sat in the prison room, pushing the food around in our bowls. I always stretched out my mouthfuls. The food was fresh and abundant, and mealtime was the main distraction of our day. I picked up rice and bitter melon on my chopsticks, taking time to appreciate the food that had grown on vines and in the rice paddies surrounding us in the fresh air, the farmers that had watched over them like they were as fragile and mercurial as their children, waiting patiently until they were ripe enough to pick them then delivered them to the market down the road. I appreciated the vendors who sold these things, the cooks who had gone down the market to buy them for us and then came back and prepared them. They used good recipes. They took care in their cooking.

I admired their thoughtfulness, how they could take pride in feeding us well.

When I popped some fish in my mouth, I recognized it was cá tra, but I didn't shudder at how its plumpness came from our own waste.

"Even cá tra is not so disgusting anymore," I said to Quoc.

"It's more disgusting to think about Thông having sex with his girlfriend," Quoc joked.

My brother giggled, still sounding like a little kid.

"Before taking a shit outside the rice paddy," Lan, another close friend, added.

The old man laughed. He seemed to be aging faster, staring at nothing in particular with a faint smile on his face. Other guys noticed, too, and were kinder to him.

The locks on the door shook. It was the police chief, standing there with his shiny shoes.

He looked around, disoriented at first. How pitiful we must have looked, our dirt-streaked faces, the open sores on our behinds, our collective stench. Although we tried to take care of our space, dirty underwear and shirts and books were in piles around us.

"Thanh," he said quietly. "I am going to be off tomorrow night. Please wait to continue your story until Thursday."

I nodded, showing him that I understood. When he left, the guys reacted to the moment, their voices buzzing like an electric current through the room.

CHAPTER 24

Mom

June 1977

They escorted Thông and me into the tiny outside courtyard. Beyond the barbed wire divider, about three meters away, was our mother.

She was dressed strangely, in country clothes with black pants, a white button-down shirt, and a straw cone hat. The disguise made her resemble a Southern farmer. My mother usually wore perfectly pressed dresses and suits, Western makeup, and coiffed hair.

Her face was devastated at seeing Thông's scrawny body, even though I'd done my best to clean him up that morning. He still looked tragic, like a baby bird who had fallen from the nest.

My mother stood stunned, taking in the enormity of what had happened. Seeing her there brought it all back, memories that I thought I'd discarded along with my clothes on the road. I remembered our house in Saigon with its big cool high-ceilinged rooms, the food on the China plates on the table where we sat on chairs and ate every day. I remembered her serene face when we were in the sitting room with my father and he told stories about their fun but rough early years.

A picture emerged in my head of my mother standing in the beach house, holding one hand on her rounding belly, the other hand holding mine, which was stretched up high to reach her, a rare gesture of intimacy.

Was this memory real? Had my mother been pregnant with Thông?

It was only then I realized that I was crying, tears streaming down my face like a slow-moving insect.

As if on cue, Thông started crying. Then my mother started crying too.

That was the strangest part. I wasn't used to my mother showing any emotion.

The tall guard stood there, his expression bemused. I hated him more than anything at that moment.

"Are you okay?" my mom asked.

"We're okay."

There was so much I wanted to tell her, to explain how I'd done my best and followed the plan. I wanted to tell her how sorry I was for messing up, for not protecting my brother and ruining our chances.

Thông started tugging at her arm like an infant. His clothing was threadbare, covered in yellowing stains.

"I tried to keep him safe," I whispered.

Her forehead creased in confusion and pity. Had Tám Điệu told her what happened? Did he blame me and Thông for getting caught?

"It's not your fault, Thanh," she said in a soft voice.

"But I didn't—"

She stared at me harshly. "It's not important. We don't have much time."

I blinked my eyes to show her I understood.

It occurred to me how far my mother had traveled to come visit us, how much danger she faced just by riding the bus. There was always the chance that she'd be stopped and questioned about her trip away from her hometown.

But I trusted my mother's capabilities. I recalled how she handled the household after my father had left—accumulating gold bars, securing foods not included in the rations, purchasing the plot of land to pretend to have a reason to be traveling, arranging for our transport to the South.

"The family is okay," she said. "Your dad has been transferred to the North, and we haven't heard anything from him since. Your brother Thinh and his wife plan to visit your sister. We are working to do all we can to get you out of here."

Relief flooded me. My mother was telling me in code that Thinh found another connection and would escape soon to be with my sister in California.

"I brought your favorite foods, like pork stew and dried shredded pork," she said and gestured toward the bags the guards were holding. "I brought your guitar too. Thach told us," she added.

Guitar. The word sounded magical to me. It was something out of the serial stories.

Suddenly, the guard touched my shoulder. His grip was firm, not mean, but told me the visit was over.

"It's okay, Thanh. I am so happy to see you," my mother said.

The guard started leading her away.

"*Mother, will* you come again?"

She turned and stared at me then slightly nodded. There was sadness but determination in her expression. I know she would bribe the right people and get us out.

CHAPTER 25

Memories

The room was heady with marijuana smoke that I was almost stoned before I pulled the joint to my lips. It had been rolled in thick tobacco leaves. I inhaled deeply, like I had smoked a few times with friends in Saigon. The country plants were stronger, and I started to choke.

"Take it easy there, Saigon. This weed isn't for babies."

I started laughing. That made me choke more.

"That's good stuff!" I exclaimed, trying to salvage my dignity. Everyone laughed.

It was already dark in the room, but I was starting to see pin-pricks of color.

"Sometimes we were right out there in the field, under the stars when even in the night the ground is so warm. Still, I don't want to smush," a guy said. His name was Giang. He was a typical Southerner, local guy who smelled bad when he sweated but had a real gift for telling dirty jokes and stories. We all liked to hear them.

"What girl? Is she skinny?" my brother said in that sweetly embarrassed way he had every time we started talking about sex.

I turned to see my brother with the joint in his hand, looking at it curiously.

"Thanh, show him how it's done," someone said.

Everyone laughed.

I turned to see my brother with the tobacco leaves in his hand, looking at it curiously, the same way he had when they gave him a cigarette.

I showed Thông how to take a drag. I imagined my mother would be disappointed.

Thông took a drag and passed the leaf on. He smiled at me, his grin so wide.

"See, the kid knows what he's doing. He's growing up," somebody said.

"Learn from your brother, Thanh."

Everyone busted out hysterically then, sounds that sheared through the sky like ocean waves, like the undercurrent of wind. I couldn't disentangle them. It was such a beautiful night. I loved the whole world so much that it ached.

Giang was telling a new crass story about a village girl's house he'd sneaked into when she gave him the signal. He had lain next to her half naked under the mosquito netting

"And everything is okay. It is good. I am kissing her sweet skinny neck, and then I nibble so gently on her earlobe, you know, just that right spot that makes her moan, and I know it is okay to move in closer, you know. I'm ready."

As he described his climax, he banged on the floor with his hand for emphasis. Laughter trilled around the room.

"Not like the whorehouse in Saigon, huh, Thanh?" somebody said.

I remembered that time. It was the middle of the day when a class was cancelled and we decided to go there, following Chan, my high school classmate who had been there before. It was a poor, dusty town. Houses with tin roofs lined the potholed roads. Pregnant women stood on sagging porches. Barefoot kids had run alongside our bicycles, calling us Brother and Uncle, offering us directions to different whorehouses.

"Oh, yeah. The women were beautiful," I said. "They stood in the waiting room in silk nightgowns, and we got to pick. You didn't have to be charming. You didn't have to work for it."

But the truth was, we did have to work hard. We didn't know what we were doing. In Saigon, we never touched girls we liked. We didn't even kiss them. We boys got our sex education at whorehouses, and the poor women had to teach us, telling us how to get undressed and where to put our hands.

I recounted one night at the whorehouse when a raid happened.

"It wasn't a real raid though. The local police would do it for show. To alert customers, there would be a warning. The kids, the watchers, the pinboys, they would all bang on pots and pans and scream. It happened this one day when we were inside one of the houses. We heard the warning and ran out onto the street naked, carrying our clothes."

Everyone started busting out then. My head was so heavy from the weed, I was laughing hard, so much that I thought I might explode. But then a thought crossed my mind that saddened me. That whorehouse raid felt like so long ago. We were so carefree, so young, the way we had run down the street howling.

* * *

It had been several weeks since I started telling the Chinese serial, and it was coming to an end. I felt the same sadness I recalled as a kid back in Saigon when I realized a serial was ending. There was something depressing about how the ending demanded the reader leave the mystical world of the imagination and return with a thud to the disappointment of ordinary life. In Saigon, that meant long hours alone in my room until it was dark enough to go out into the streets. To visit my friends or see Thuy. In jail, the end of a serial meant a return to a reality of constant agony, our bodies covered in dirt and sores, our muscles always cramped.

Although the guards were treating me nicely, I was worried. Everyone was relying on me for entertainment. But what would happen if that ability was undependable, if I lost my voice or forgot a thread of the story?

"Yes, you were telling about Phong Tu Nuong when she got in trouble. When the servants told the villain that she was coming to steal the sword."

I cleared my throat slightly and resumed the saga. Somebody moaned. I noticed the guards standing patiently in front of the window for me to resume. I went on for about thirty minutes.

I was tired, my mind knotted from talking so long. But I had to reach the ending. So I conjured up a dramatic and upbeat heroic finale from my mind. But I added a message about the deception of chasing after things that only deceive and disappoint.

When the story finally ended, everyone remained silent for a while, meditating on the message and fighting their regret. I guess they were all imagining being in the story, as Tiêu Thập Nhất Lang rescuing Phong Tu Nuong or sleeping with her, or as Phong Tu Nuong fighting to avoid being caught. In the next room, some guys started singing a sad folk song. Some women's voices from other rooms joined them, so the song became almost joyous.

The lock on our door banged. I looked up. The mean chubby chief of police came in with the thin tall one.

"Tomorrow, take one shackle off both Thanh and his brother Thông," he said quietly. Then he walked out.

CHAPTER 26

A Thousand Years

September 1977

One day in jail is like a thousand years out free.

That saying circulated around our room. It was an inside joke. It was also a truth.

After the first few months, the boredom became more irritating than our discomfort over bed sores or bug bites, the dirt that had thickened on our skin. The energy that had lain dormant in our bodies during the long days while we baked in the heat came out in the cooling night. We used to entertain ourselves with items brought from relatives, like Chinese chess boards for tournaments, notebooks to write stories or songs.

In jail, it was important that we entertained ourselves. Only one man lay by himself. He was a short muscular man whose eye twitched when he was nervous. Eventually, I recognized him. It was Hai, the Tám Điệu connection in the market.

"Don't be fooled by that guy. He works with the undercover police," the old guy with one arm whispered to me.

I explained that I knew him. I recalled how Hai had barely looked at us before as we slinked through the crowded market and stopped at the stand.

I thought about Quoc and Lan and the forty or fifty other people from Saigon who wound up at the jail because somebody had scammed them, who Hai had led the military to us. He was part of the game.

"Why is he here with us then?"

"Maybe he did something wrong. Maybe not. It is better not to know."

I knew that Hai heard us, that he was trying not to look up. We didn't know why Hai had been arrested. Still, there was a measure of justice about him being stuck in a room with men and boys he'd betrayed.

Had Tám Điệu tricked us too?

I remembered my mother's visit, the way she had looked when I told her I did my best to keep Thông safe. Had she known that we had been tricked? Was she looking at me that way because she felt guilty for sending us to Tan Dieu's house?

Late one night, I was wide awake. The air was too stuffy to breathe. I thought about Tám Điệu. I remembered how he had treated me as an equal, telling me dirty jokes. How smooth he was, charming everyone from prostitutes to men in suits with his silky voice that night we slipped down the long country road on our scooters, how we'd watched him through the window lounging at the table and being served by the beautiful girl. Those people he was meeting were not the resistance. In the end, Tám Điệu was just an ordinary con man who traded us for some gold.

I listened to Thông's breath beside me, as I did every night. He sometimes gasped in the middle of sleeping before his normal rhythm returned. It unnerved me.

It was my fault we were in Chau Phu Jail. I had been so gullible to trust Tám Điệu and Hai.

There were so many times I could have stopped it. If I had just realized sooner. We would.

I saw Tám Điệu's face again, the way his cheeks flushed when he told a story. I wasn't angry with him, exactly. But how could a grown man betray us and send two teenagers to jail?

We might never get out. But Hai did. He was released after a few weeks.

CHAPTER 27

Brother Six

It was dark by the time we started our nightly recital.

Brother Six was the guard on the night shift. Unlike other locals who liked listening to the notes, the soft opera country music from the South, he liked the modern music I played. Ever since my mother brought the guitar, it had become a cherished friend. The chords I strummed resonated in my chest, returning life to my body. It was exciting to play this strange, sweet Vietnamese music.

"Sounds good, guys," Brother Six said.

I smiled. Brother Six was a good man. He continued to offer us small kindnesses, like giving us more time by the water, even occasionally bringing us treats from the market. He took a special interest in my brother and me, making sure we had what we needed.

Now we shared another connection. I was teaching him how to play the guitar.

Brother Six had gotten permission to take me to an old bunker made of sandbags in the yard that served as a music room. We used ammo boxes as chairs. It was closed with no windows, and the air was dense with humidity in there, but there was no stench. It was such a privilege to be outside, to be holding a guitar. It gave me such a feeling of freedom that recalled my old life, before Saigon had fallen. The guitar retained memory, this thing that was once such an ordinary part of our lives, that I had left sitting in the corner of my room without touching it for weeks at a time. It was now something precious, soon would be forbidden.

It was so familiar to hold the guitar between my legs, to rub my calloused fingers against the chord and strum, coaxing sound from its belly. Even though the E string was loose and it needed to be tuned, it responded exactly as it had when it was in my bedroom.

I had a notebook in which I had scribbled instructions for Brother Six to learn to read music. I watched as he hunched over the guitar, fingers on the chords, warming up with the scales. Then we worked on the music the guys had taught me, the slow and elongated notes reverberating against the bunker walls. We practiced for hours. It was like being lost in the space of a sweet dream, where you aren't quite sure if you are awake, but it doesn't matter.

* * *

We still hadn't been officially charged or sentenced. As days dragged by, I learned to emulate the old man who sat cross-legged on the floor every day, meditating. Maybe we wouldn't find freedom in this lifetime. Maybe it awaited us in another lifetime.

I decided to hope for simpler things. If we had to die in jail, maybe I could escape the everyday boredom if I just had something to do.

I had learned to temper my hopes. Every day, guards read off the list of the few guys lucky enough to do the labor outside: to get water or work at an abandoned rice paddy. I tried not to listen. I was still a city boy with a puny body and no knowledge of simple country chores. I had earned my keep telling the stories and teaching the guitar. But the guards treated my brother and I like cherished pets.

I had grown accustomed to being passed over, so I didn't hear my voice called one day.

"Thanh," the voice repeated sternly.

I looked up from my notebook. It was Brother Six.

"Yes, you, Thanh. Do you want labor work? Hurry up."

The morning sun was beginning to bathe the rice paddy field in reddish light. The water was clear. The roots of plants and rocks on the bottom were exposed. It lapped over the field.

We were traveling to work on a rice paddy. It was a rare gift, being so far outside the camp in this massive field with one inch of water locking in patches with all the green plants.

The warm air caressed my cheek. There was an absence of human noise. The birds, bugs, and other creatures were singing to each other in odd buzzes. Their humming restored me.

We fixed up small rice paddy walkways along the vast field. My feet were up to my ankles in cool water. The water lapped. It was so beautiful, it physically hurt.

A memory returned to me. It was 1976, right after the war ended, when I was introduced to Thuy. Our group went to the beach town Vung Tau. I recalled the water caressing my bare feet and the gentle presence of Thuy as we were walking alone. We didn't talk. There was something so peaceful about that long and sweet silence.

I missed her so much.

I walked over to the edge of the field. There was no water there. The sand was dry. I used my big toe to write *Thuy and Thanh*. I looked at the big clumsy letters. I hadn't known how much I had loved her until that moment.

I swept my whole foot across the names, feeling its coarseness on my soles, and wiped them out.

CHAPTER 28

Old-Timers

We walked with police escorts in the front and the back. It was stunning to be breathing real air with my feet moving upon the ground.

When we got to the market, we saw villagers at open stalls in straw hats and wide-legged cotton pants. Vendors picked up watermelons and mounds of water spinach. Fishermen weighed pounds of fresh fish and shrimps. Cheerful voices echoed in the warm air.

This was the market where the cooks obtained fresh food which they cooked into tasty dishes that weighed in our bellies. The people in the market occasionally glanced up at us. They had been instructed not to talk to us. We were not an unusual sight—filthy and bug-bitten barefoot guys with sores all over our bodies. We headed toward the canal with our buckets and sticks. As we walked past it, I again felt connected to the ordinary world and was filled with an immense sense of gratitude.

When we were returning to the camp after walking down and up the canal to get water, we were disoriented. We stood there in our boxer shorts and naked chests, our arms holding a long bamboo stick precariously balanced behind our necks and skinny shoulders. We had padded our pants and shirts over the shoulders to keep the pain minimal.

The buckets were light before being filled with canal water. They were now like lead, making our necks bob and our knees buckle.

Like everyone else, I was concentrating only on keeping the buckets in the air and from falling down. My jaw locked from the exertion.

At first, the guards barked out orders as we stumbled and sloshed water all over the ground. Then we realized they were laughing at us. Like most of the guys jailed, we were city boys. None of us had ever hauled water before. I was able to see the absurdity of the situation and held back my own giggle.

It was the third time we had been out, and I was just starting to get the rhythm of walking with the buckets, making sure it didn't cripple my body. My body had gotten stronger from the fresh air and exertion. The other guys were getting it too.

We passed over the main road. Below, we could see the open market, the stalls and bodies moving through. There was a village beyond. The regular world was still there, a contrast to that dark cramped room where our legs were gnashed by cuffs.

When we finally got back to the jail, we were smiling. We had a welcoming committee of guards and prisoners from the South and were in jail for nonpolitical reasons, either caught stealing or being vagrants or getting into a fistfight on the street. They cheered us as we made our way back to camp.

The candle illuminated the tiny room. We'd gathered in a semi-circle, my brother and me and our friends from Saigon. We still had our chains as we leaned over a little wooden piece the guys said they got from a casket in the graveyard.

We were playing a magical game that Quoc and Lan knew. The board could connect us with the dead. It was called a Ouija board.

On one end of the board, we wrote in the word *yes*, and on the other side, *no*. There were characters on the other parts of the board. We cut the piece of wood into a triangle, a heart shape that would guide us. My brother had his fingers on the triangle, along with another guy from Saigon.

"Will we be released this month?" my brother asked.

The triangle started moving in a slow creep along the board.

I gasped. I didn't usually believe in those things but couldn't deny what I saw. At the same time, the good student in me knew this was impossible. And besides, if the spirits could help us, we would have been released a long time ago.

But I got chills, which pushed up my arm hair. Something felt electrified in the room. The triangle moved across the board to the *yes* letters. Someone made an eerie sound and people laughed, but nervously.

"You moved it," my brother said, laughing. It was good to hear him laughing again. Both the rash and his leg wound were practically gone. He was acting like his old self.

"Nobody moved it. It's not us," someone else said.

"When will we be released?" Thông asked. "What date? In the next few weeks?"

"No, no, you can't do it that way. That's too specific," someone said.

"When is my mom coming back?" asked Thông.

"Thông! That isn't a good question," I said.

"Let him try," someone said.

I sighed. It had been months since my mother had visited. If she had managed to bribe the right people, it would have happened already.

"Okay, when is my mom coming back? Thanh, what is mom's name? What did you call her?"

I watched as the piece on the board moved dramatically to the right, where *no* was written.

I lay back on my sleeping mat, my head cocked back on the makeshift pillow. They had released all the women and started to release some of the guys. When we first started playing the game, I couldn't believe it. But now it wasn't inconceivable that there might be a day when they let us leave this place behind.

CHAPTER 29

My Brother's Freedom

It was early morning when the guards started coming through the yard. They carried lists and began reading out names. We heard the women's names first: Nguyen Thu Ha, Nguyen Thi Ngoc Lan, Tran Thi To Anh, followed by high-pitched exclamations. It was the second day they had started to release people without explanation. Most of the women were gone.

When they approached our room, we tried to act unconcerned. A couple of guys began to gather their belongings.

"Dang Tran Vu. Nguyen Tuong Thông."

"Thanh!" my brother screamed out as relief rushed me like canal water. My brother's name was soon lost in a new list of three names.

"Get your things. You have five minutes to pack," the guard said.

"Thanh, why didn't they call you?" my brother said.

"It doesn't matter. They called you. Get packed."

Those on the list were excited, slamming things around as they packed.

"Thông, you are going back to Saigon, right?" a man asked. He had not been chosen. He asked if my brother could deliver a note to his family.

I helped Thông pack, muttering instructions as they came to me.

"Don't talk to anyone. Take the buses straight there. You remember how to get back to the house, don't you?" Thông nodded in response to my barrage. Then he collected all the folded pieces of paper that prisoners were pushing at him. His face was beaming, his black eyes moist. I took out the outfit he had been wearing the day we were captured, the only real clothes he had left. I helped Thông into the clothes then started to comb his hair with my fingers like I was his mother. He pushed me away, laughing.

"Hurry outside. Now!" a guard barked as he opened the door.

"Go!" I yelled at Thông, giving him a clumsy hug. He looked at me sheepishly, then left.

Locked back in our room, we looked at the new freed people all stood out the window, squinting through the barbed wire.

There were at least fifty standing out there. The guard called off each name and gave them papers and a little bit of money. One by one, they walked toward the highway and the bus stop. Thông was among them, dressed in long pants and a short-sleeved shirt and sandals—clothing that looked formal after months in shorts and shirtless. In one hand was a small bag. In the other, his papers.

He looked slightly taller to me. Or maybe it was just the proud way he was standing. He had been through so much in those eight months. He had suffered, but he had also grown.

He turned toward me and waved, a huge smile spread across his face.

A tear dripped down my face. I could breathe again. My brother was going back home.

CHAPTER 30

Don't Hope for It

It was early morning. Everything sounded differently in the room because there were only six of us left.

The camp had emptied out, and there were fewer guards. But we had a new concern: with less supervision, it was more likely they could hurt us.

So when the door opened abruptly, we all flinched. Nobody spoke. We waited until they had unlocked the pole and our legs were free, our calf muscles pulsing in our legs.

"Pack your things and come out into the courtyard," one of the guards said.

"What's going on?" one of the guys said.

"Today you are going to be released. We transport you to another camp first, you fill out paperwork, then you can be released."

* * *

The young angry guard spat as he tied rope around the wrists and elbows of four of us prisoners. We were standing in front of the big Russian trucks. He yanked so hard our shoulder blades curled backward.

"It's not a good sign," one of the guys said.

Like everyone else, I wanted to believe what they told us, that they were preparing to release us. In the brown-green truck adjacent to us, ten more guys were sitting, their arms tied. Some were beam-ing, as excited as a child during Tet. Others looked confused.

The guard pulled the rope again. Somebody moaned.

"Hey, don't be so rough," Brother Six said and pushed the young guard away. He loosened our ropes so that the sharp blue pain in my shoulders began to fade.

He squatted in front of me and looked in my eyes.

"Don't hope for it," he whispered.

CHAPTER 31

The Crane

There is a myth about a crane who has lived out his one thousand years on earth and, while on route to the afterlife, gets caught in a rice paddy field so vast he cannot find a way to fly out.

Ta Danh, the green watery labor camp we were transferred to, reminded me of that myth. The camp was on the border of Vietnam and Cambodia. It was treeless. Any direction I looked in mist blurred into the horizon. Dense land bled into the sky. I'd never before seen a place so flat and endless.

It was difficult to tell in what position the reeducation camp was fixed, if it was in the center of nowhere or on one of the edges. A sharp fifty-foot-high bamboo fence locked us in.

They pushed us through the gate into an enclosure hemmed in by barbed wire. I looked around for Quoc and Lan but couldn't find anyone familiar. I was all alone now. We moved toward the seven long narrow halls pressed together with only a few yards of space in between them. They were built crudely, thatched grass woven rooves strung by perpendicular bamboo poles over a structure made of wooden slats made of bamboo and other reeds from the jungle. These were fitted loosely together with spaces in between that let the sun and rain in, gaps that would serve as our window.

They moved us, hunched slips of guys with sore wrists, into a cluster of yellow bamboo barracks with thatched roofs. A guard holding a rifle stood in a high tower.

The long ride had cured us of any illusion that we would be freed. I was almost, but not quite, resigned to my fate, to the deep understanding that my life was no longer my own.

The men herding us into the area were brusque but unnervingly quiet. My arms still ached from being tied behind my back the whole ride. It was difficult to breathe. The air was soaked with humidity.

It had finally happened. The edges of the dream had blurred. All the things I'd experienced until now were just a confusing rush of fading memories: the travels, the aborted escape, the arrest, the jail cell, the promise of release. And now, a labor camp. It was like those watery patches of land I could still make out that seemed to be both anchored and detached. Once, my brother and I walked outside our motel room, quietly eating stewed shrimp on the street in a strange land. Then we were in a jail cell with our legs stuck to a pole, telling stories as a kind of a prayer. Here I was in the land the crane got lost in, far away from my family and home.

I missed Thông. But being alone loosened the burden of responsibility. I was grateful my brother was safe. I was now responsible only for myself.

I don't know how long we'd been standing there before the sky cracked. The rain was warm, tickling my ear, my forehead, my collarbone. I arched my back, hoisting my bag on my shoulder. I watched the rain. Then I turned and looked toward the distance, the blotted sky splashing the muddy fields. Was this better than eight months I'd spent in the clammy jail?

I stared at the rain and saw figures slowly emerge from the mist. I stared so long until nothing became something. It was so gray out there, so unclear, it took me a while to understand. I saw first their legs, then their hips and their chests, and their arms and their heads. They were emerging out of the mist, out of nowhere really, like ghosts from another world. So many guys, maybe a thousand, mud slathered on their faces and arms. They'd been out there all along, invisible while squatting down at work in the paddies. They were running in groups of a hundred, herded by camp police in yellow khaki clothes.

They advanced quickly. I saw them more clearly. How wiry some were, how short, how skinny, with smooth jawlines. Some were teenagers. It was oddly comforting to be around young people again.

"Keep moving!" I heard a guard shout out. As the rains increased, people jostled more quickly to reach the indoor barracks.

They moved us in groups of fifty. We were all weak from hunger and exhaustion, our bodies twisted from months of being chained. We were eventually pushed into a large hallway with two open decks. Each side of the hall was lined with double-decker bunk beds where hundreds of men lay shoulder to shoulder. In the center was a narrow walkway, which we learned to utilize to set up chess boards or play music.

Animals were penned in better conditions. The humidity was unrelenting. The stench of dirt and unwashed bodies became ever present, like the stench of well water we were given. We had to wait for the sediment to settle before drinking it. The guards' conditions weren't much better. Their thatched-roof barracks were outside, where they slept under mosquito nets on thin mats.

I tried hard to get my bearings, like the lost crane who was trapped in its vastness, who was on route to eternity, who sought release from the earth. We were imprisoned and supervised by faceless men in uniforms the same color as mud. I wanted to burrow in the ground and go to sleep before my mind gave over to insanity.

"Hey, you, Guitar," I heard a guy call out. He was the room captain, Hung, a gangster-like guy whose roughness contradicted his handsome appearance. He yelled orders at all the kids. He didn't seem like a mean guy, more like the older cousin who kept all the young guys in line.

I realized I'd been holding the guitar at my side. Music was the one thing I still had that I loved and was able to hold onto. The guitar tugged at that hopeful place deep inside me.

I saw the way the room captain was looking at it. I remembered how much freedom the guitar had earned me at the jail, how it had won the guard's affection. That led to my leg cuffs removed and ultimately joining the outside work crew. I decided the guitar must have magic powers because my mother brought it to me.

"Guitar," he repeated in an angrier tone.

Before I knew what was happening, he'd grabbed me by the shirt and hustled me up a flight of stairs. The room captain pushed me into the corner.

"Set camp up here. You'll sleep near me," he announced with finality.

That night after eating, they locked us in the barracks. I had set up my sleeping gear between the wall and Hung, with my backpack between the guitar and the wall. Hung was huge, one wrist like two of my own. He had a habit of blowing air out of his mouth, like smoking a cigarette.

"This spot is good, Guitar?" Hung said.

"It's a good spot," I said.

"Tomorrow you will play for us."

I was glad he wasn't going to make me play that night. I was so tired from the long ride.

But everyone else who arrived with me was still awake and playing. The room had the feeling of home when my brother was babysitting and he let us stay up late.

Four young guys squatting on the floor were playing Chinese chess near older guys, gossiping and playing cards. Some other guys were singing low, cracking jokes and laughing.

"Everyone here is so young. The last place I was in, there were mostly old guys."

Hung nodded.

"You were at Chau Phu Jail before Ta Danh. How long?"

"Maybe eight months."

"Was the food good there?"

"Yeah."

"Most of the kids are here for small crimes. Kid stuff. Stealing food for their families. Fighting in the street. Getting drunk." He laughed. "It isn't so bad," he continued. "You get the food and bed. You do the time, usually three to six months. Then you go home. Some come back again and again. Maybe they like it."

Across the way, one guy was running around the room and whispering in everyone's ear. Everyone started laughing, slapping him as he passed them.

"You are different, city boy," the gangster said. "You aren't here because you stole." Then he walked off without letting me respond.

I reached for my backpack and unzipped it. My khaki T-shirt was in there. I had hidden it instead of having it stamped with *Reeducation* like the rest of my clothing when I checked in earlier. If I ever found a way to escape, I could wear that shirt to ensure freedom.

CHAPTER 32

Hard Labor

It was 5:00 a.m. We stood outside in a line, the morning sun just beginning to peek out of the sky. Even though the dorms were damp, I'd slept well, my body huddled under blankets.

"Move," it sounded like the guards were saying. I followed the other guys past the courtyard. There were yellow khaki police surrounding us.

We walked a dirt path across patches of soggy land, built up as border walls to keep the rice growing correctly. I was disoriented by the warm air tickling my cheeks and by the hooting sounds of strange birds.

I didn't know where we were being led, but a momentary happiness surged for the ability to walk in the fresh air. It felt more natural, somehow, to be among other young people. The fact that none of them were political prisoners and most had release dates made me feel hopeful that I would be treated better than in jail.

I was surprised at how long we walked. An hour later, we finally stopped in a wide-open area in the rice paddy. I could see the sunrise. There were sectioned-off work areas and a massive irrigation canal, about fifty feet wide and mysteriously deep, that curled out for miles. I stood there, amazed, as a yellow khaki officer was barking orders.

The next thing I knew, guys were running toward some destination. I paused, my feet in the mud, unclear what they were doing, and then I followed them. They all grabbed shovels on the ground. I guessed they had been left there from the night before, and all the

100

guys were racing toward them, somebody checking each other and jostling them away or diving to retrieve a tool.

I stood there, like a fool. I understood that there was a hierarchy of the tools, that some were better than others, but I didn't know if the tools belonged to specific people. I waited, staring at one of them which was a strange shovel with a two-foot-long handle, one and a half feet long with a very sharp head.

After everyone retrieved a tool, I picked up one that was left. I watched the kids plunging shovels into the earth, pulling up huge blocks of mud, and then tossing it far, twenty or thirty feet back. I didn't want the police to notice my ignorance, so I tried to imitate the guys.

The first time I put the shovel into the earth, it bounced off it, like there was rock under there. I finally found the right place to plunge in, but my biceps were too weak to lift it. Guys laughed at me, but in a good-natured way, and some offered advice.

It astounded me that we were forced to build a canal with our shovels.

Even if my body wasn't so weak from jail, it had never been strong enough to do this work like country boys. But I tried. I learned to balance the mud on the shovel, but I couldn't throw the mud as far as everyone else. My biceps ached.

By the end of the day, about 3:00 p.m., everyone stopped their work, and the police inspected the work. We had a quota, a certain number of cubic meters of canal to dig out every day. I hadn't completed my quota.

"You are not finished!" the policeman yelled at me. "Pick that shovel back up."

I started working more. My entire body was knotted, my back hunched. Sweat streaked my face, and I felt my chest was about to explode.

"Nobody will leave here until Thanh has finished his work," he announced.

By the way the guys started to laugh, I knew this wasn't the first time somebody failed a quota. But it didn't make it less humiliating. The embarrassment kept me focused so I could work faster. I tried to ignore the mounting pain every time I plunged the shovel in the muscles in the back of my neck, especially, and felt like I was tearing the muscles.

A half hour or so later, my shirt sticking to my back, I didn't feel like I'd made any headway. I saw several coworkers were restless, hungry, and probably angry at me.

"I can help him. I'll do part of his share," one guy offered.

"No, he must do it himself," a policeman barked.

"Nobody leaves here until he has finished his obligation," another policeman said, a sharp smile on his face.

I plunged the shovel in, deep into the earth, determined not to let them defeat me.

CHAPTER 33

A New Friend

Hoang lay next to me in the hall. I liked him because he was close to my age. He just started talking as if we had been friends all along. He had a big head and short legs. He spoke a lot, but softly. Most people didn't have the patience to try and understand him.

Hoang was in the camp for something petty, like most of the guys. That was what made us different. He knew his release date. But it was quite a long sentence. We political prisoners had no idea how long we'd be stuck.

"When did you get here?" I asked.

"Just a few weeks. I hate it," Hoang said.

"I love it," I joked.

"I was at a different camp before. Nui Cam, Forbidden Mountain, on the border of Cambodia. Only kids, no adults. It was better."

"How?"

"The mountain was the trap. It blocked us anyhow. We had a lot of freedom. We could do anything we wanted as long as we did our work. We could walk around the village. The work wasn't so hard. I want to go back there."

"Oh," I said.

"This land is a trap too. They can see you everywhere. There is nowhere that you can run."

He was silent, then exhaled sharply.

"This place is too strict. The work is hard," he said.

"I'm getting more used to it," I said.

"I can't stand being locked up. It makes me so mad. I can't take it."

He was silent for a few seconds.

Down the hall, I could hear other guys laughing and playing Chinese chess and cards. I felt differently than Hoang. The work was tough, but it was like paradise compared to the jail. I thought about describing it to him. About our legs chained to the wall in the dark, the sores on our buttocks, the stench of lying on filthy mat. But I was too embarrassed.

"I just wish I could go back to Nui Cam."

Sometimes, wishes were strange. It hit me how different Hoang was. There was a sweetness about him, an innocence. Perhaps because he was from a family of farmers.

"I will tell you a secret. But you can't tell anyone," Hoang said.

"I won't."

"I'm going to escape," he whispered.

"You can't do that."

"Why not? It is easy. Someone made it."

The fields had been guarded on two sides by guys in the yellow khaki. The previous week, a guy had escaped by running down the middle. We had watched the whole thing. The guards shot at him, but he was too fast.

"Yes, but they are watching closely now since he escaped."

"I know a way."

"This is an empty place. So flat. It doesn't matter which direction you go. You are always in their line of sight."

"I am small, and I can outrun them."

He was quiet for a second when the chatter in the room dropped. He waited until it picked up again to continue.

"A few miles away, there is a river. And if you cross that river, there are villages. If you get past the villages, you can go wherever you want."

* * *

The rain had become part of the fabric of our lives. It soaked our clothing and hair and softened the land. I came to think of the rain as good because the climate was pleasant.

I was standing in the dorm, watching a soccer game in the courtyard. The kids were running barefoot in the mud from one end of the court to the other. I'd been pretty good at soccer in high school, but it was tiring just watching them.

"Hi, Thanh."

Hoang was standing there, dripping wet and his feet muddy. He had a big mischievous smile on his face.

"Oh, you played soccer? Was it fun?" I said.

"Do you like soccer?"

"I couldn't imagine playing here. After working all day, I am so weak."

"I'm tired after work too. But I play soccer so I can build the strength in my legs so I can run faster."

I knew what he meant.

CHAPTER 34

The Yellow Khaki Shirt

When I came back to my spot, there were big blankets on the edge of the bed. I kneeled and felt the first one. It was pilled and rough but thick. I felt the second one. It was the same. Hoang suddenly was at my side.

"Do you have anything to trade?" Hoang said.

His mouth was pinched in a mischievous smile.

I imagined the weight of the blankets on my body, how nice the heat would be. It was raining a lot, and the nights had been cool. The bamboo structure was drafty. I'd been waking up nearly every night shivering. Sometimes I didn't get back to sleep. The next morning, exhausted, I found the shovels too heavy.

"You are serious, huh?" I asked.

Hoang nodded.

Now that his plan was real, we wouldn't speak about it aloud.

I thought of the endless expanse of the field that Hoang would have to travel through, the guard in the tower with his rifle trained on his back. I didn't have that kind of courage.

I went to my backpack that doubled as a pillow and pulled out the unstamped khaki shirt. I lingered as I crumpled it in my fist—my only chance at escape—and passed it over to Hoang.

"Here," I said, putting it under the single blanket he had left.

It was a long time before we spoke.

"It's not stamped," I eventually said. "This is yours now, okay? Don't ever tell anybody about this shirt."

"I promise."

* * *

It happened one day, just after lunch. I was standing in the field with the shovel in my hand, the scent of the mud strong as I dug. The sun beat my back where I hunched over, under the vapory blue sky.

There was a sudden commotion. Guards were screaming, their angry voices clawing at the sky.

Gunshots rang out.

I dropped my shovel. I put my hand on my chest.

The guards rushed onto the field as we lined up. Rumors spread quickly down the line of hundreds of us. Someone had escaped, running away with guards in pursuit.

I knew it was Hoang.

I thought of him that night when he gave me the blankets with his cute mischievous expression.

I can outrun them, he had said.

I imagined him getting to the edge of that field, to that river.

Go, Hoang. Run. Keep running! I screamed in my mind.

I imagined him wading in the river, crossing over, reaching the villages.

The guards finished the headcount and hustled us back to our jobs.

Later, back at camp, the guards locked us in our barracks.

We each lay on our bunks, peeking out of the gaps between the bamboo slats. A group of forty police and guards in yellow khaki were running into the camp, whooping and hollering.

I stood there, praying.

I had pushed my face into the bamboo. The rain fell hard on my skin.

The way they ran, hoisting their guns, and the way they screamed, there was a violence about it, a cruelty to their celebration. It stunned me. There was another noise, a kind of a celebratory noise, a magnetism, like the way the thousands of birds all descended on the paddies at once. This noise was foreign. Yet it was familiar.

I peered out into the field. Two guys were carrying something tied up to a bamboo pole. Then I noticed the length and weight of what they tied, the way that it hung. I made out the feet then, the calves, the knees and thighs. It was human.

They opened the gate and marched into the courtyard with the body, parading it around so all of us could see.

It was dead.

I couldn't breathe. My stomach was chorded with knots.

It was still raining.

Eventually, they got close enough that we could see. One of the guys at the pole was using his hand to keep the head held up. Then someone handed him a towel because the man's brains and blood were spilling out of his head. He was using the towel to try and cover it up.

The guy had been shot in the head.

It took me a few seconds to look. I saw his yellow shirt. The top half was soaked with blood. I realized it was yellow. And it hit me, as I turned my eyes down, that was my khaki shirt. The boy who was wearing that shirt was my friend.

The guards circled around with the bamboo pole, joyful expressions on faces slicked with mud. Then they turned around and marched the body through the back of the camp, through the gates, and back into the fields.

I pressed my face against the slats in the bamboo as the rain pooled on the thatched roof then dripped down and into the walls. I felt it trickling on my forehead and falling on my cheeks, mixing with my tears.

I stood in the field by the canal later that week, trying to piece together what had happened.

Hoang, my friend, had run pretty fast. So fast that the guards couldn't catch him. His time spent building his muscles from soccer had paid off. But the guards had anticipated his escape, so they had stationed men at the river. It was a trap. They shot him right there, on the spot.

He didn't have a chance.

I thought about Hoang, about his simplicity, the way he had spoken about escaping, the way he'd wanted to go back to forbidden mountain, to his other camp.

There had been nothing political about Hoang. He was just a farmer. He'd only wanted to go home. And then they paraded his corpse. What kind of people would do that?

CHAPTER 35

A Pit Stop
Chau Doc City Jailhouse

I sat in the Chau Doc jailhouse on the blanket and pillow I had traded with Hoang. I felt like it was the most heavenly place that existed.

The massive cell was clean and cool, built from white stone with a thick cement floor and red brick roof. I shared it with about thirty older guys. It was late morning, and we were eating a decadent breakfast of real rice and local fish that had been cooked in a smoker. The best part about that jail was the water, clear city water that came from a faucet. Water that you didn't have to wait until the sediment settled to the bottom to drink did not torture our stomachs and bowels.

I had been writing a letter to be delivered to my family. I hadn't been in touch for six months since I didn't know if I should ask them to visit me. Our existence was nebulous; authorities never told us how long we'd be staying at this prison.

I looked out the window. The morning sunlight flooded the long stone courtyard where the water was piped to a large water container and a large bathing basin on the ground. Some inmates said this courtyard used to house a guillotine built by French colonizers to execute resisters. The guys had finished their breakfast and were lounging in cotton pants, squatting over a chessboard. I wonder if they realized how much of a luxury this leisure time was.

In this jail, we did absolutely nothing but wait. My muscles had grown firm from digging canals and doing hard work at the labor camp. I now had a rare time to relax.

Another beautiful thing about being in the city jail was sanitation. Everything was so clean. We had showers every day. Every prisoner had scrubbed faces and unstained clothing. When I scraped my fingernails over my arm, there was no longer any dirt. There was only the faint scent of stone and mud.

This way of living was more familiar to me. I was from the city. My mother dressed in silk áo dài to go to the market. The housekeeper made us kids scrub behind our ears until they were red. This city brought me a sense of peace.

The guys were friendly enough, but I didn't feel like interacting. I had lost too many friends since we'd been captured. Like Thuy and my other friends from Saigon, Quoc, Lan, and other Saigon friends in Chau Phu Jail, then the twenty guys from the jail who I recounted the Chinese serial stories to. Hoang was the biggest loss. The brutality of his death had shaken something inside me, so I was afraid to interact anymore. At the same time, I wanted to stay in that jail forever, drinking clean water and eating real rice. Hoang would have probably liked it, and he wouldn't have run.

Some nights I sat up and thought about Thuy. I remembered the crooked way that she smiled when I told her a joke about how much wisdom there was in her silence. More than anything, it was her gracefulness that I loved. Thuy was the only one who I trusted actually cared about what I was saying and could almost understand. I thought she could understand even the last year of my life, or if she couldn't, that she would have listened. I often imagined what life could be like if I was ever released, how I would recite to her certain details, mostly the funny stuff. I thought she would be amused to know how my Chinese serials had saved me, how I had written her name in the sand. *I thought about you often,* I would say. *Our memories saved us.*

It hurt me to know that I would never have that chance.

Other times, I thought about Thông, out on the streets looking for his stewed shrimp. I thought of Thinh teaching me how to love the music. I thought of Dad telling stories on the last day he was at home, his disappointment in watching me smoke. They were kind ghosts that wandered through my daydreams, my night dreams. It had been nearly a year that I had been shuttled between jails and camps. When I imagined Thuy and my family, it was the only time I didn't feel alone.

CHAPTER 36

Message in a Bottle

There is a certain kind of exhaustion that occurs when you no longer control your own body, when you are being transported as a captive from one place to another. All day long we sat on busses, our wrists and ankles slugged with rope. They did not tell us where we were going. We only knew that we were not free.

I watched the landscape changing out the window, as if in a dream. I felt each pothole in the road shudder through my bones. Oddly, the closeness of the other men comforted me. It offset my feeling of vulnerability. I ignored the officers with guns surrounding us. They were only minor annoyances. I saw the vegetation on the roads, the houses we rolled past where people must have been doing ordinary things—cooking rice, sewing, making cassava. The indeterminate nature of our destination didn't scare me.

After about six hours, I realized we were moving north. My mind grew agitated. When our convoy of ten buses rolled into Saigon, I woke up. I became acutely aware of how closely we were tied. I struggled to keep my body from shaking, squinting back the tears in my eyes. I'd been gone less than a year, but it felt like a lifetime.

The busses passed through the streets.

I saw places I remembered. I remembered the feel of a busy street with small alleys. People pressed together, women haggling, wooden scoops plunging into vats of rice and mung beans. I saw two men sitting on crates playing chess. This was my city. They had no right to take it from me.

I tried to get a whiff of hot city air through the open window. Everything was constricting my chest, like I was wearing a too tight T-shirt. A sadness pulsed in me. I missed my old life. I missed my family. The tears burned my face.

But I was glad that Thông was released. I imagined him safe at home with my mother. I imagined the five brothers and my mother who were left, sitting at home eating food around the table. Had it been easy for my brother to return to the ordinary ways of doing things? Of sitting and eating and sleeping? I tried to imagine the rooms of the house, the big living room, the bedroom where I read my books.

We headed toward the center of the city where the streets were wider. Traffic clogged the area. As I watched, I also realized that my binds on my hands were loose, even though my arms were tied. I kneaded the knots, pulled a loop looser and looser, then began tugging at the end with my other two fingers. I realized the streets would get more crowded, forcing the buses to stop, blocked by giant crowds. This was my opportunity.

I was in the row close to the front of the bus. A cop, a slight man, was staring blithely out at the crowds, paying no attention to us. His rifle was at his side. I imagined myself sneaking to the front of the bus, pushing him aside and rushing out then disappearing into the chaotic crowd.

We stopped at a light near the market. The stalls were over-flowing with hanging meat and fruit. People were spilling out of the narrow alleys. The ropes were completely loosened on my arms. I went over the plan again in my head. After I pushed through the doors, what would happen if I got stuck in the crowd? And then if I managed to run, how would I find my way back to my family? Wouldn't they look for me there? If I didn't get to my family, where would I stay?

The bus rolled deeper into the market, toward another rush of shoppers. I saw poor women holding bags of cabbages with babies on their backs. I saw old men with grimacing faces. I imagined myself standing up, pushing, running, but I couldn't move. The plan wasn't sound. Could I run fast enough to escape? Would there be police on the street? What was I going to do in Saigon without paperwork?

These thoughts slammed against my mind, paralyzing my body. The bus moved away from the bustle. I watched with my lips parted as the driver moved through the streets, as everything seemed to change to slow motion, get quieter, smothered, as if the bus tires were wrapped up in cotton or cloth.

By the time the bus stopped at Tao Dan, a large municipal park, disappointment stabbed me. I'd missed my chance. The park was practically empty, save for some poor people sleeping on benches. We were stopping for fuel and a rest.

The park sweepers approached the bus curiously. They knew we were political prisoners and that we were on their side. The cops screamed at them to back off.

A few guys on the bus began to yell out the window.

"I am Nguyen Van Dung! My family is at District 4. Tell them I was on this bus. We don't know where we are going."

"I am Nguyen Bien Duc. My family is on Pham Ngu Lao Street."

"Shut up!" the police yelled.

Nobody moved.

We were at the stop for a long time. The cops returned to the front. I noticed some guys had gotten their ropes off. One had gotten paper and pen from his bag and was writing a note. He crumpled it into a ball and catapulted it out of the bus window. Other prisoners did the same thing. Paper balls were falling on the ground.

I loosened my ropes more and managed to unhook my back-pack. I reached in and got the pen and paper I always kept, from the time I first left Saigon. I opened the notepad and began scribbling.

October 1978, Tao Dan Park, Saigon

This is Thanh. They moved us from the jail.
Don't visit me there.
I am well. I am healthy.

115

We passed through Saigon today. I don't know where they are taking us.

I ripped the letter off the pad and folded it. Then I scribbled my family's address on the top of the folded page.

I looked around. My heart surged as I found another clean page. On it, I wrote her name.

> For Tran Thi Ngoc Thuy
> Address

I picked my pen up. I felt this would be the most important letter I ever wrote.

> Dear Thuy,
>
> I am here in Saigon.
> I miss you.
> I have been captive for more than a year now.
> I don't know where they are taking us.
> Keep in touch with my family. They will let you know.
>
> Thanh

I held both notes in my lap. When the bus started moving again, the guys started to crumple their papers and throw them out the window. I crumpled both papers then carefully pitched each ball out the window. I turned around to watch the street sweepers collecting the white balls.

Hope surged inside me. It didn't matter where we were headed. Thuy would get the note. She would forgive me for that night at the party.

CHAPTER 37

K-3 Labor Camp

We climbed to the top of a red hill, facing out to a gigantic mountain in the Central Highlands. The busses let us out. We marched through the gates. The barracks resembled the barracks in Ta Danh. But these roofs were made of tin or sheet metal instead of coconut leaves. The walls were cheap wood instead of bamboo. I counted at least twenty of these barracks.

As the prisoners came off the bus, I heard bits of conversation.

"This is a big camp."

"Arid. The air is dry here."

"No young kids. There are more soldiers, doctors, intellectuals."

"The elite. That's what I heard."

Until now, I had just tuned everything out. But these sounds were familiar. The men who were walking with me up the hill were speaking in my Northern accent. There was a sophistication to the way they put sentences together.

My body relaxed. Some fellow prisoners were from Saigon. They sounded educated. I had spent years in the South with guerrillas and farmers who made fun of my accent. Now I was no longer alone.

The rain had started back up. We were surrounded by huge redwood trees, and it was cooler up there, almost like our heads were touching the clouds.

"Form an orderly line and file into the hall. Constructive physical labor. Xuan Loc K-3, Z30A labor camp. "Obey these orders and nothing…"

The obnoxious voices from the loudspeaker were familiar too. They sounded just like voices from our neighborhood.

We were hustled into a very large hall, several hundred men of us, standing side by side. It had high ceilings and was constructed with great care and sophistication. Several huge solid round wood logs supported the inside of the structure. There was also a stage.

Guards stood with severe expressions, planted at each of the walls, dressed in dark yellow short-sleeved uniforms. They wore yellow hats with red flag emblems on their collars. Red and gold ribbons were stitched across the length of their shoulder blades.

I stood there with the papers they had given me. I had finally been formally charged of escape. And a sentence of three years.

The chief of police on the stage had been talking for a long time, the gold buttons and stripes on his sleeves moving up and down as he spoke.

"You were lied to. Deceived. Brainwashed. You were lackeys of the American henchmen. The imperialist oppressor. You are not here for punishment but for reeducation."

I looked out the window to the steep hill below, its trails leading to a valley and fields.

"Your time here will not be easy. But it will be rewarding. Constructive physical labor. Purged of the lies."

This labor camp was huge and organized compared to the others. I thought about some of the horror stories my relatives from the North had told us, how hard they worked to get my father released from a labor camp. They had not been successful.

"Nothing is more precious than independence and liberty. When victory is won, we will rebuild our land ten times more beautiful,'" the chief of police said, quoting the late Ho Chi Minh.

"Freedom is ours, and already we are rebuilding our beautiful land. A place where everyone is equal, where everyone gives and receives according to their needs and abilities."

There was a gonging sound in the distance. Three times it banged.

"Already our GDP is soaring," the chief of police continued. "You are fortunate enough to be a part of this new society."

I looked back out at the window. Coming up the hill under the pouring rain, there were hundreds, maybe thousands, of bodies. Men covered from head to toe in red mud. They all had their heads down, this army of red ghosts.

CHAPTER 38

My Surrogate Family

When I was a child growing up in Saigon, I never could have imagined that one day, the idea of eating a termite queen would make my mouth water, that I would try in vain to snag that gelatinous morsel stuffed with sweet eggs from the center of the insect's giant clay house. The delicacy was afforded only to the strongest guys at K-3 Labor Camp. Among the youngest, I was a nineteen-year-old kid with jutting hip bones even before being captured. I had to be content with barbequing the occasional lizard or frog.

"Are you dreaming? Wake up," my friend Quang said, snapping his fingers.

"Why? It's a nice dream. I got the queen for once," I said.

Quang laughed his dry wheezing laugh.

We were near the barbed wire where we dried our ragged clothes on the top of Phuong Vi, Royal Poinciana, the name of the flower our hill was named after. As we peered out over the valley, to our right was the dense green jungle beyond the wire. There lay the path leading into the bottom of the valley. That path was like a red waterfall, a line of guava-colored dust that zipped up the hill's bright green body. Behind it was the warm olive silhouette of the Chua Chan mountain.

"Have some water. You're going to need it. Big d…day today." Quang said, a slight stutter to his speech as he shoved his Guigoz can toward me.

We were about the same height, though his hunchback made him a little shorter. Quang was about four years older than me. He'd been a college student when Saigon fell but had a babyface like I did. I admired the way he still kept his short dark hair well-groomed. He slept in the next bunk, and we ate meals together. He was my closest friend.

"Take it," he insisted.

Quang took my hand and placed the Guigoz can in my grip. I took a sip, swishing the warm water in my mouth and then swallowing hard. A wave of dizziness engulfed me, the kind where my bowels threatened to give out. It had been happening all day. I leaned into a tree and put my free hand on it to balance. I concentrated on breathing through my nose, my face flushed.

Quang studied my agony for a second, looking at me with an odd head cocked, the poetic way he examined a silky corn husk or deer poop or the sunrise. Quang didn't live in the same world as the rest of us guys at the camp.

"Are you homesick?" Quang asked.

I stared at him. The word *homesick* made no sense. Nobody at the camp believed we'd ever leave for home again. And it had been nearly a year since my mother had traveled all the way to the country to visit me. There was no such thing as home anymore. But a tenderness in Quang's voice tugged at me. Quang was sensitive. He listened deeply.

"Thanh," Quang said quietly.

The sound of my own name already sounded strange to me.

"It's so clear out there. Beautiful. Take a look," he said.

I looked into the valley below. Women worked the farmland, carrying bundles of wood on their heads. Cooking smoke drifted above the thatched roofs. Down there was family, real life, freedom.

"Don't be so stubborn. You are no good to us if you get yourself blown up," Quang said. Then he laughed hysterically. He was teasing me. It was the first termite mound I'd been assigned to clear. Clearing the mound was the most dangerous job at the camp.

I looked down the hill toward the dense jungle. Gnarled plants competed for light. Sticky vines climbed stumps. Roots spread furiously under the earth, undermining ancient hardwoods.

In the center of the plants was the long clear field we had spent the month preparing with our machetes and hoes. We were getting them ready for planting corn, cassava, and peanuts. Our work would provide food, barely sufficient, for the three thousand former scientists, doctors, soldiers, lawyers, and politicians in danger of starving to death.

Just beyond the edge of that field was the fifteen-foot-tall red clay mound the termites created out of their spit and tenacity for their queen. We would soon be dismantling it.

Quang and I were positioned in the place where our people, the Army of the Republic of Vietnam, ARVN for short, had base camps during the war. The termite mounds jutted above the bamboo and shrubs and provided good hiding spots for the Vietcong and Communist forces. That was the reason the land around them had been rigged with land mines. Approaching the mounds required great vigilance.

"Is your hoe good and sharp?" Quang asked protectively.

"Yes," I said.

Our hoes were a source of personal pride, one of the few possessions we were allowed to keep. We lay them in the fields at the end of the day and reclaimed them the next dawn. Their sharpness could determine whether we worked smoothly or we injured our backs toiling. The mound was the ultimate test.

A few months before, a man tripped a mine. It was soon after lunch, when the dry air squeezed the saliva from your tongue like water wrung from a washcloth.

While chopping stalks, we'd all heard the explosion and felt the loud boom in the bottom of our shoes, so strong we could practically taste the metal in our teeth, feel the shrapnel in our own heads. The sensation never left my body.

"Then there is nothing to worry about," he said.

"I'm not worried."

Quang walked over to me in a way that reminded me of Charlie Chaplin. I had seen the comedian on the black-and-white television in our living room with the American soldier who rented a room in our house during the war. I remembered how tiny I'd felt among the giant man.

Sometimes, I felt just as out of place at the camp. The majority of guys had been in the military and had seen combat. I wondered if those guys had been toughened before they'd gotten to the camps, if that somehow helped them.

I looked at Quang. Like me, he'd never really been in the military. Somehow, after Saigon fell, he was involved with the underground resistance, was captured, and wound up at K-3, a few years before me. Despite his nervous manner of speaking and his funny walk, people trusted him.

"Anyhow, you will love it. You aren't going to believe the place where the queen lives. It's like a spaceship. If you are lucky, you will crack it yourself and get to eat it," he said.

"I won't get the queen." I smiled.

"Why not? It happened in your dream," Quang said.

The air was dry and the hill quiet. There was a chattering sound in the distance coming from behind the trees that could have been a human or wild animal.

Quang began to sing, in quiet, halting English.

"When I find myself in times of trouble…hmmm…how do the words go again, Thanh?"

I smiled. I knew what Quang was trying to do. Here at Phuong Vi, in the place where the future was forbidden, memories of our past could keep us alive. My memories were guided through song. I was a popular rock and roll guitar player in camp, and playing yellow music, the kind Communists forbid, was an act of bravery.

Under the circumstances, it was the best I could do.

"Mother Mary comes to me, speaking words of wisdom, let it be," I sang as low as I could.

Just then, a guard began howling at us to get back to work.

* * *

I stared at the guys' feet. Sixty feet, many of them with thick crusted nails and deformed toes. All wearing sandals we wove out of salvaged rubber truck tires. All sunk into the red dirt. The feet were side by side in a long line stretching from the mound to where the guards stood in the shade, wearing puke-colored uniforms and funny spherical-shaped Communist hats.

I raised myself up and looked at the mound. The gargantuan red dome-shaped termite house looked as hard as concrete. We were dwarfed by it.

The heat was a haze that wavered in the air like grease over a grill. That air, perfumed with the sap of rubber and redwood trees, stung our nostrils, as did a rush of small bugs. Sweat dropped from our foreheads into our eyes.

Some of the guys were excited to start the attack on the mound. I'd noticed myself how I'd started changing inside, becoming more primal. The previous week, I'd watched a group take the body of a guy who'd died from malaria down to the cemetery. For the first time, I didn't dwell on how terrible it was.

For some guys, walking over mine-rigged land was a way to feel a rush of endorphins, a break in the monotony. It caught their minds with the same excitement of meeting a beautiful girl. I was not one of those guys. The fistful of dry gritty cassava I'd eaten for lunch came up sour in my throat. I swallowed it back down.

The guard barked an order. We advanced. We tread slowly, with practiced steps, sweeping the earth with long hoes, slashing the ground to look for mines.

And in my hour of darkness, she is standing right in front of me.

We worked in unison, felling the tall trees first and then the larger ones. We cleared the ground to eventually let new things grow. We got closer and closer to the mound.

Speaking words of wisdom, let it be.

In the distance, the guards were shouting, a mechanical sound somewhere between encouragement and disgrace. They would yell when something was accomplished, as if they had to prove they weren't slacking off, sitting in the shade and chattering.

Let it be, let it be. Whisper words of wisdom, let it be…

The song stopped as we made it to the mound, men clapping each other on the back in encouragement. We no longer were in danger of getting blown up by a land mine.

Still, there were other dangers hacking a termite house to bits. The mound was so hard, the hoe often bounced back and smacked us. We knew what else awaited us—thousands of termites furious that we invaded their sanctuary. Plus an equally angry collection of snakes, rats, squirrels, lizards, and larger insects.

"Don't low, don't low, placate!" the guards barked, urging us on.

In our row between Quang and me was the strongest among us, a tall, fit, dark-skinned guy. We called him Ms. Dan because he sewed and cooked as well as any woman. He was a people pleaser, always volunteering to help others carry water or start fires. Even though he never had a visitor, he always wound up eating meals with the richest guys at the camp. It was a selection process as intimate as marriage. Even the guards liked him.

Ms. Dan was a mystery. He'd graduated college with a degree in political science, but he rarely spoke about his past.

We knew Ms. Dan would likely get the queen. We also knew he would do the most strenuous work, using a delicate force to swing his hoe while we were breaking our own backs.

Personally, it didn't matter to me. I was content to gawk at the treasures inside the mound. I was still a city boy at heart, and the sights of the jungle still astounded me.

My shoulders ached with every swing of the hoe so bad they were nearly cramped. The impact made my knees turn to jelly and made me want to cry. Even though I wouldn't be the one to get the queen, I kept swinging, getting lost in the rhythm, until we broke through.

Two Cambodian guys, jailed for joining the resistance, ran off chasing a large green snake. When roasted, it would taste like leeks. I'd watch them roll its slimy, bloody body against their bare backs because they believed it would strengthen their health. Another went after a squirrel, always impossible to catch.

The termite mound insides were hollow. It looked like a futuristic city with cavities, secret tunnels, and passages linked together by the spit dirt. Insects were scurrying about, crumbs on their backs and things in their mouths, traveling like harried pedestrians in a city.

We focused on the center and the ultimate prize, suspended by bobbing clay strings. It was a thick rounded dome with holes and windows that looked like a spaceship. It housed the thumb-sized queen, her plump body stuffed with hundreds of tiny eggs.

Sure enough, Ms. Dan reached in and cracked the ship with one chop to expose the queen. He dropped the hoe and reached his hand in, beating out two others who were grasping wildly, ignoring the thousands of tiny red creatures that covered them, stinging. He pulled out the queen, his arm swarming with the tiny red insects.

"Ms. Dan's got it!" someone screamed.

He opened his palm and dropped into his mouth the globular white queen, which burst and popped. He swallowed.

We cheered and laughed. Ms. Dan cleared off his arms, and we all returned to work, flattening the rest of the mound.

CHAPTER 39

To Live

A dozen men sat in a circle inside the barracks. Smoke rose in the center of the room, twining up from an iron teapot. An oil lamp burned, casting shadows on our faces.

Behind us, men were laid out side by side on coffin-sized mattresses, their mosquito nets draped and zipped. One guy, sleeping in the dirty, low-status section beside the latrine, was snoring.

It was a sweet, dry night. The air had cooled enough that the fecund scent of the scrub outside was carried to us by the wind. That scent could make guys feel connected to the spirit of life beyond our painful conditions the way that incense burning at a shrine in a temple once could. A few guys squatted near the door, boiling tea out of crushed roasted corn and a new blend of mountain plants. It smelled pungent, smoky.

The guys sitting in the group were all my trusted friends. The poet Tha sat on his rump on one side of me, his back hunched like a tortoise shell from the mortar that had permanently lodged in there. His eyes were glassy and fixed on the air in that mesmerized way that he had—always slightly removed from the world.

Beside him was the guy we called Tin Địa. That was because he had a big plump belly like the earth Buddha they kept in shrines in stores. He was the only prisoner who wasn't all muscle and bone. We couldn't understand how he got fat on a daily handful of cassava and the occasional kernel of corn or insect. Chubby Tin Buddha always seemed to be having the most fun.

Tin was about three years older than me. He held himself with a kind of soft-spoken confidence I lacked and a worldliness that most of us longed for. Tin was college-educated and had become a helicopter pilot, trained in the United States and served in the ARVN. He amused us with stories of the American truck stops where they used to eat something called fried chicken and pick up giant blond women. Most of his family had fled to France long before the war ended. When his mother visited, she brought him decadent foods like French chocolate and coffee, which he occasionally shared with us. He chose to hang around with other college guys. I envied his sophistication. Even though few of us had any hope that we would be freed from the labor camp, Tin made us feel close to our dreams. If he could do it, anything was possible.

"Look at that smug guy, still bragging because he got to eat the queen," Tin said, laughing at Ms. Dan. Ms. Dan's expression was both glowing and bashful.

"He's looking all satisfied, the way I look after with my girlfriend," Đầy said. He was a good-looking macho guy, constantly rolling his sleeves up to show off what was left of his muscles.

A few guys chuckled. We were all used to Đầy's romantic tales. Most of the guys had embellished the beauty or purity of their wives or girlfriends or lovers for us. Some of their stories were like newly lit candles, a flickering flame they protected while watching it slowly burn down.

Tha didn't speak of women with such grace. He could get raunchy. He often bragged of their impossible lust for him. Tha had been a courageous rebel fighter and was probably very attractive before he got caught in the bomb explosion. We had no mirrors to show us how ugly starvation and hard labor had turned us. Even though Tha's wounds were proof of his bravery, they were also a permanent reminder of how different he was. He couldn't get up in the morning without feeling his deformity.

"She has long beautiful hair and a beautiful body. She has this way of kissing that is so sweet."

Halfway through the story, one of the guys pretended to fart. We all laughed hysterically. Behind us, the snores got louder. The expression on Đầy's face darkened. He was one of the best storytellers in our group.

The room went silent for a few polite seconds. Something screeched outside, a bird or jungle cat. We heard them at this time, big animals with padded paws and heavy treads that the guys rarely could put a name to.

"Did I ever tell you guys about the time I saw that kid down by the river? He was so young," Tha asked.

"I'd like to hear about it, Tha," I said.

Tha cautiously picked up his metal can then took a long sip of the tea. Then he stared back into the cup before putting it down, giving the silence a long time to settle. Steam rose in front of his face in the darkening lamplight.

"I was only a private in the Marine Corps. I was young, maybe a few years older than Thanh there. We were in battle way down by the border. Afternoon. Heavy shelling. Loud. One of those days when the sound of machine-gun fire can make you go deaf. It replays itself in your head, like the chorus of a song. You know how that is, right, Thanh?"

He paused and cleared his throat. He arched his body, ribcage to back, and stretched. Then he began.

"We were in the mountains fighting. It got rough. But there was a break. There is always a break. Both sides need to recuperate. The human body can only fight for so long. It always happens that way. Some folks think it's because you need more supplies, but that's not true. It's just the way it works.

"I was thirsty. I walked down to the stream to get water. My mind was burned out, exhausted. I was walking in a dream to this stream that led out to the river.

"Then this guy comes out of nowhere. A soldier from the North. I noticed how young he was. The skin on his face was so smooth. His eyes were young. An innocent kid who still doesn't believe there is bad in the world. But he was the enemy. He was just as shocked to see me as I was to see him.

"Neither of us moved right away. We just stood there, staring at each other, smelling each other's crabby breath. There was a muscle on the side of his eye, like a vein, that twitched. I don't know how long we stood there, but it felt like a long time."

Somebody moaned in agreement. Tin took his cup and gulped loudly then put it down on the ground.

"Then it was like I woke up, like somebody had clapped their hands. I just reacted. I was supposed to. I picked the gun off the ground. He was so close I had to take a step backward to shoot so it didn't kick back."

Tha paused.

"He died. If he wasn't so young, maybe it would be different. If we hadn't been so close, we would have just been two guys at a stream, getting a drink. Some nights, while I am trying to sleep, I can see his face."

Nobody spoke right away. The oil lamp had almost burned out, and the guys' faces were fading. More had filled the beds and were heading to sleep. The older man, Hong, was standing in the corner, sneaking his last smoke with pungent pipe tobacco. He began a dramatic booming coughing fit that sounded like he was going to die right there. We laughed.

That night, I lay in my bunk. I thought about Tha's story. It wasn't so much the words but the tenderness in his voice. Unlike most of the guys at the labor camp, I had never picked up a gun, let alone been forced to shoot. But I felt I could imagine what Tha was feeling when he saw the bullet rip into the enemy.

I had noticed something similar when the North Vietnamese had arrived on our streets, dressed in jungle clothes. They scrutinized our houses like they were spaceships, the same way I'd later regard the corn growing or termite mounds. I'd recognized it then, the strange theatrics of war. They were like singers at the Saigon Opera House, awkwardly maneuvering in their heavy costumes across the stage according to someone else's direction. Most of us didn't know who we were fighting or what we were fighting for.

CHAPTER 40

New Lunar Year

February 1980

It was Tet, the three feast days that marked the new year and beginning of spring. It was the only day we were allowed to stop working. For those three days we were granted a reprieve, the opportunity to feel part of the world. The holiday raised our spirits. We sat around the courtyard, our hearts heavy, longing. Guys who I'd never seen look up, even in the barracks, were staring at the sky, gap-toothed smiles on their thin faces. Occasionally, one guy touched another's arm while they talked. Laughter buzzed, like little kids who had broken the rules in grammar school.

We felt more human because our bellies were full with exotic foods. We had real rice instead of cassava. They had slaughtered three pigs and boiled them into a rich stew, which was divided among a thousand guys. Those foods made us feel cared for, valued.

The guards left their posts on these days. Smoke from cooking fires rose along the hillside.

We imagined our loved ones were probably celebrating Tet too. They would be dressed in their best clothes, visiting the temples with our neighbors and cousins.

Some camp guards were not resentful of our education, the prestige we had before Saigon fell. They tried to learn some things from us. Some secretly took guitar lessons from guys in the orchestra, even learning yellow music from the Western world. Some guys even made homemade instruments like guitars and flutes from tree limbs and hardwoods from the jungle, using strings from the black market.

I was one of the youngest guys in camp. I'd gained the same popularity for guitar playing as I had at Chau Phu and Ta Danh. They liked my bravery in playing yellow music, songs I'd memorized from the Beatles, the Rolling Stones, John Denver. Sometimes, when the guards or antennas weren't around, I would sneak off with others to play forbidden rock music in some corners of the camp.

The other prisoners at K-3 had a different kind of bravery than the guerrillas and farmers I knew in the other places. Many former soldiers had served in the military alongside American soldiers, and so they loved the same rock and roll I did.

One guy stood out. Ly was half Chinese. He had come to the camp a year after I did. He'd grown up wealthy and had the good looks of a successful playboy. Before being captured for joining the rebellion, Ly had been a famous drummer who'd performed in night-clubs before the war ended. He was immediately inducted into the orchestra.

I wasn't surprised, then, when I heard his name buzzing electrically like a current of insects in the air of the courtyard.

"Thanh, get your guitar. Then come to no. 2 barracks," I heard. Someone said that Ly would join us.

Dozens had started to gather in the barracks. Someone had made a stage, and musicians stood on it. There was a guy with a bass, a few guitars, and some strange instruments. Father Chuong, the camp orchestra's conductor, was beaming and waving his conductor's stick. Ly lugged his entire drum kit onstage and was warming up.

I was pushed up to the stage and stood between Ly and Father Chuong. I lifted my guitar, my fingers playing the right chords. The audience grew, and more guys started making their way onto the stage with instruments. Suddenly, it was like the whole camp had gathered, hundreds of guys crammed shoulder to shoulder.

We played a song by the Beatles. I was swept up in the sound of the music, playing maniacally, the sweat dripping down my back. We had never played with drums before, much less a famous drummer like Ly. Happiness surged through every guy who was standing in that forbidden room. We could have been anywhere at that moment, at a house party, at a club.

As we played, I was energized by all that I did, the way I arched over the guitar, the way the chords vibrated, the way my fingertips rubbed against the strings until they ached. One of the guys was crooning a mournful French dirge. For a brief moment, I felt the momentum in the room drop, as if we had gone too far. Then the drumbeat took over, and a new song began.

"Thanh."

I looked up, my head still bobbing like a crazy guy on stage.

"'Hey Jude!'" someone screamed out. "Thanh, play 'Hey Jude.'"

Ly began drumming the melody, and others followed with guitar. I looked at the Catholic priest in the crowd for permission. He nodded, waving his hands in the air.

Hey Jude. Don't make it bad...

The strange American words were difficult to form. My voice cracked at first, but with Ly keeping the beat, we got stronger.

Take a sad song and hmmm it better.

The guys all started laughing and whistling and screaming, cheering us on.

Remember to let her into your mmmmm...

I didn't know any more words.

"Then you can start to make it better," a guitarist screamed.

We limped toward the final lyrics.

"Na na, na," the drummer started.

"Na, na, nana na," I picked up, calling the audience to do the same.

"Na na, na nana na na ana," they echoed.

My voice crooned in a pitch that I'd never imagined could come from me. The guitar chords, the undercurrent of the bass, the pounding of the drums echoed through every nerve ending in my body, cleaning me out. My voice bellowed.

"Hey Jude. Jude, Jude, Jude," I started.

"Na na, na na na na na na," the audience all sung. People hooted and hollered. They whistled and cheered.

The sweat dripped from my forehead to my collarbone. I was smiling so hard, I couldn't believe it. My body was on fire, cushioned in the endorphins, the collective voices of the guy echoing inside my rib cage.

"Na na, na na na na na na."

"Hey Jude."

It was one of the proudest moments of my life.

The next morning

I sat in the courtyard with some guys. We were still off work, but things were uncomfortable again. Lots of guys sat with downcast eyes, trying to make themselves invisible. The joy that I'd felt the night before had been replaced with fear.

"They took Ly and Dat, the one with the homemade guitar," Quang said. "For question...ning," he stuttered. "Others too. At least five guys."

Quang was squatting, the hunch to his back like a turtle shell. He didn't look concerned.

"I'm not worried," I said and smiled.

"Some just got warnings," Quang said. He groomed his newly cut hair with stubby fingers.

"It was worth any punishment," I murmured. Across the courtyard, two guys were playing cards. Another was sloshing his clothes in a vat of water. A third had raised a needle toward the sun and was attempting to thread it.

Quang smiled shyly at me to suggest he agreed. The jam session was the most fun I'd had since I'd arrived at the camp, the freest I had ever felt. In Saigon, I could have never imagined one day I'd be singing the Beatles to a crowd full of screaming people, that the shy guy would become a rock and roll star.

At the same time, there was no way my performance went unnoticed. There would be consequences.

I looked around the courtyard, trying to figure out who was the antenna that reported us. They had also questioned the conductor, Father Chuong.

Quang made a long sound like he was whistling, piercing into the silence. He bounced slightly into a more comfortable sitting position.

"They sent some to solitary. Probably just a few days."

Solitary. I remembered when a man escaped then was put into that cement block for several months. How he looked hollowed out and haunted when they finally let him out of solitary. I'd often glanced over at him in the field and noticed his expression, how the sun seemed assaultive to him. Worse than that, there was something hollow in him, in the mechanical way he lifted the hoe.

There is meaning in life, even here.

I thought of the conductor's gentle eyes, the way he had found meaning to survive here for so many years. They wouldn't keep him confined for too long. He would be okay.

CHAPTER 41

Remembering Thuy

After you live long enough as a captive, you come to value modest things. A sugar candy that melts into syrup on your tongue when you are starving. A lost note of music. The cadence of a forbidden poem. Thuy was the one thing I held most dear all those years.

Thuy was everything I held precious, delicate, sacred. She was as elemental as her name—pure water that washed over me, absolving me of every humiliation I had endured.

The moments our group gathered together around the coffee stands at night were some of the greatest I'd ever known. They were more remarkable, because although it was a secret between us, Thuy liked me better than any of the other boys.

If life hadn't changed the way that it had, my memory of Thuy may not have assumed such importance. She would have just been a girl I once thought was cute and lost track of at a party.

* * *

The sun pressed down on my back as I hunched over, slicing my hoe into a knee-high stalk and working to clear the jungle field. I turned to examine the ball of flame in the pale blue sky, just above the deep olive of the mountain.

The sun's placement meant that it was about 4:00 p.m., that hour when the air made my tongue feel like water from an old washcloth.

And the guards were being stingy with our breaks.

I pressed my bucket hat firmly on my head. I raised my hoe then brought it down like a sword, jabbing at the plant's tough roots. I took good care of my hoe, sharpening it almost ceremonially, but that day, my actions felt futile.

"How was your visit with your mother, Thanh?" Quang asked.

Quang was one of the few guys at Phuong Vi reeducation camp who had never been a soldier. He often rebelled against his internment by slacking off.

"The visit was fine," I lied.

A wave of dizziness rushed me, the kind where my bowels threatened to give out. I stuck the hoe on the ground for balance. I reached for my blackened metal Guigoz can on a stump. Inside, there were only a few swallows of water left.

I wiped the sweat off my forehead and got my bearings.

First, I reminded myself where we were. The field we were leveling to plant crops was on the halfway point of Phuong Vi, the hill the camp was named for. More than three thousand prisoners lived there, hemmed in on both sides by the lush rotting plants, which hid the barbed wire.

"It's cooling down," Quang said.

It was not cooling down. The heat wavered in the air like grease over a grill. The perfumed sap of agar wood and pine hung in my nostrils.

"If you stand still enough, you can almost feel it."

"Feel what?" I asked.

"There is the slightest mountain breeze quivering from behind," Tha, who stood nearby, chimed in.

I kept swinging. I had no patience for Tha's poetry.

"I'm looking out," Quang said.

My bicep started to twitch from fatigue. I repositioned the hoe closer to the root of a stubborn shrub, making short quick stabs. I hit a rock and repositioned again, swinging harder. The scent of old wet earth rose up.

"It is like your guitar playing, Thanh. The way vibrations hang in the air," Tha said.

"There is no breeze," I replied, trying to sound mean. I turned from Tha and continued to work.

The plant loosened, and I threw my hoe on the ground then yanked it up, short gentle little yanks until it started to budge at the roots.

A memory of my old girlfriend, Thuy, returned. She was standing on her parents' veranda, a dim bulb silhouetting her in the night. She had dragged her long dark hair over her shoulder, revealing the delicate bones in her neck and her chest.

"The guards are all the way down by the hill. Relax," Quang said.

Her name formed in my head.

Thuy.

The dead returned to us at strange moments. Memories slithered in like lizards, never stopping too long. We chased memories in the same haphazard way we chased animals, guided by the primal instinct to fill the hollowness in our bellies and hearts.

And it had only been a day since I found out Thuy was gone.

"It's almost time for break anyhow," Tha said.

I stopped swinging for a second, but only to be polite. Tha was only two or three years older than me, but he was more childlike in the way he avoided work.

"You see," Tha said.

I looked down the hill where the guard chatted with an armed guard.

Quang smiled at me, showing the poor condition of his teeth. His forehead was pinched with concern. Quang was not a troublemaker, and he had a sensitivity from being imprisoned for over five years, from weeks in solitary confinement.

"Are you sad because of your visit?" he asked.

Our visitors were allowed every three months. If they came, they hunkered down across the table from us and recounted the list of people who were gone, dragged from their homes in the middle of the night. Many died in the reeducation camps of malaria or starvation. Others, like Thuy, had drowned with their families while trying to escape.

"No, I'm not feeling like that," I said.

"Break, break," a gruff said.

It was finally time for a fifteen-minute break.

Tha and Quang left me alone, and I sat on the hillside against the trunk of a baby redwood. I sipped water slowly to savor it before swallowing. The sun had started to set. A thin breeze tickled the back of my neck. I pressed my palm on my thin pants, feeling my bare skin through the small hole I had grown tired of patching.

The water and the breeze helped. My body and mind had cleared. I felt tender again, imagining Thuy, her long dark hair tickling my arm. Her laughter was rare because Thuy was so shy, and that made it even more precious.

I touched that indentation between my throat and neck where Thuy had once touched me, just before I'd kissed her forehead. The mountains were darkening to a gray green.

I was in that sweet in-between state that Tha, the poet, always lived in, amazed by the feeling that had returned to my heart, when a white butterfly started fluttering inches away from my face. I had never seen a butterfly in the jungle.

I watched it land on a yellow sappy weed in the grass, and its wings came together twice before it pushed back into the air. It remained there, floating.

A memory returned to me. In elementary school, I read a foreign classic story about a train conductor. He was driving his train one night and still had a long shift to finish.

Late that night, the train was traveling through a windstorm. But a butterfly emerged out of the chaos and started flapping then flattening itself on the windshield. It got stuck.

The train conductor couldn't see correctly with all the rain, and the odd butterfly distracting him. He kept moving his wipers to make the butterfly leave. It worked, but the butterfly kept coming back. With the wind getting heavier and the butterfly flapping all over the place, the conductor had no choice but to stop the train.

It turned out the train was only seconds away from a washed-out bridge that had blown out over a rushing river. When the train conductor later learned of his wife's death that night, he believed the butterfly was his wife's spirit, coming to save his life.

I don't know whether seconds or minutes had passed while I remembered this story. The white butterfly did not leave, now flying too close to my head. I flicked my hand at it to try and shoo it away. It didn't leave me.

I was never a superstitious person. My mother kept a shrine in the house, but I was never religious. Still, the butterfly hovered and demanded that I pay attention.

I heard the guys behind me on the hill, talking softly, laughing. The field below was only a quarter cleared. But I didn't feel sick anymore.

I imagined I could smell Thuy's skin, the salt and yeast from her family's bakery.

The butterfly kept hovering.

I was still annoyed. But I also wanted to believe.

In my mind, I spoke to her.

Okay, if you are Thuy, let me know.

The butterfly stayed where it was.

If you are Thuy, let me know. Land on me.

The butterfly landed on my shoulder.

A warmth rushed my body. I knew it was Thuy.

Even though we were apart, there was still love.

CHAPTER 42

Angels Sing from the Sky

At K-3, Sunday meant privacy, freedom, the only day we could rest. I sat on the hill airing out the new pair of pants Ms. Dan helped me sew out of scraps.

The sun was just setting into the guava-colored valley below. The wind tickled my cheek.

The loudspeaker coughed on, a rush of white noise followed by a piercing squeal.

They never turned the loudspeaker on.

I waited for the cold authoritarian instructions. The voice never came.

I dug my fingers into my scalp and felt a clump of red clay from the rainstorm that morning. I flicked the clay on the ground.

Men's shirts and underclothes waved slowly on the clothesline in front of me.

I was enjoying the freshness of the air after the rain when strange sounds filled the air.

Music piped through the loudspeakers. At first, I just felt it, the way the vibrations entered all the places where the body met with the ground—my palms, the bottoms of my thighs.

The music was aching, coaxed from a woodwind instrument. Horned instruments rose and fell in a crescendo. I pulled my legs to my chest. I hadn't heard anything so beautiful in years.

The loud instruments leveled out and descended. Then I heard piano keys being played. It was all so unreal.

I stared down the hill at the garden where the oldest inmates worked feeding huge obo squashes and bok choy with loose shit from our latrines. These vegetables were only for the guards.

I looked beyond to the windowless concrete bunker with its iron doors used for solitary confinement. Farther down was the cemetery where we carried corpses.

The music got stronger, deeper. I heard the long soulful bowing of a violin. Each note touched me deeply. I thought about what the notes were the way that Father Chuong had taught me. There was an A, C, E. There was a long drawn-out staccato trill that reverberated.

I closed my eyes, and then I opened them. The music was floating on the trees, floating toward the green mountains. Chills rose on the back of my neck. It took me a second to realize that I was crying, the tears slipping down my cheeks.

This had never happened before.

A picture of my brother returned to me. I saw his giant sneaker again and watched him bending into his waist, grooving with the music, pretending to play guitar. I had completely forgotten that moment, that emotional connection, not just to my brother but to music.

I didn't know how much I had missed it.

I could live without food, apparently. But my heart needed that connection to music.

Are you homesick? Quang had asked me a few days before, talking about the mountains and the wind.

I finally understood what he meant.

CHAPTER 43

A Confession

I sat in a corner of the barracks, my notebook open on the long bench. It was our Sunday's lunch hour, and most of the guys were still outside.

"Show me the octaves again," Father Chuong said.

Father Chuong was about fifty, one of the oldest guys in the camp. He had been a Catholic priest during the war and refused to give up his religion. Maybe 30 percent of guys in the camp were Catholic. I never saw them praying.

Father Chuong was lucky to be placed in the camp's orchestra and got to practice and play instead of doing labor. He was talented and wrote the skits for the propaganda plays which were performed on holidays and special occasions.

I scribbled some notes on the page. He was secretly teaching me the fundamentals of Western music. The octave consisted of eight notes. All notes formed the arrangements for the vocals.

"That is close, but you have the base wrong, and this third one doesn't correspond."

My pen froze on the page.

"Try again, Thanh. You were close."

I slammed the notebook closed in exasperation.

"I appreciate that you are trying to teach me to compose songs," I said.

I knew that he cared for me because I was young, and he knew how much I loved music.

"It's just...what's the point? There is no point."

My smile could not conceal my frustration.

"What does this mean?"

"All day long we cripple ourselves with manual labor. It means nothing. There is no reason we are farming. All the lies that they tell us just to keep society stable. There is no reason for it. And they took us away from our families for all of this."

"Be careful," Father Chuong scolded. He looked around the room in case there were spies. They watched fellow prisoners and reported back to the authorities in exchange for special privileges or an extra spoonful of food.

"Thanh, one of your best qualities is your innocence. You understand how to keep your heart pure, to create."

"What is the point?" I said.

The heat in the room was palpable then. I rolled the pen in my hand.

"We are here. There is nothing we can do about that," he said.

There was a deep resignation in his voice.

I felt so petty, bringing up my small troubles. I hadn't lived like the guys in the camp. I hadn't fought for my principles. I was just a teenager who had run away and been caught.

"There is still hope for the people you love. There is meaning in life, even here."

I put the notebook in my lap and put the pen in the center of the binding.

"I have been here since it opened in 1976, four years," he said.

The gravity of his voice held me.

"More men in this camp have lost family members than ever before. This newest wave, and there are thousands, come from wealthy families."

A strange sound like a sob escaped my throat. It surprised me.

"Did you recently lose someone you love, Thanh?"

"Her name is Thuy," I said.

"A family member?"

"No. A girl. Everyone on her boat drowned."

"You loved her," he said.

Father Chuong watched with compassion as my body continued to heave in pain.

"I keep remembering her face the last time I saw her. I was unkind."

An underground party was held at the house of a friend. His parents were out of town. I was on my scooter in front of the house. On the seat behind me was a girl named Bao Quyen, her long legs wrapped around my own and her hands touching my waist.

I felt so self-righteous to show her off. Bao Quyen was two years younger than we were. Her short glossy hairstyle was copied from Western magazines. Her tight jeans flared at the bottom. She wasn't as mature as Thuy was, and she was kind of loose in the way that she carried herself. She was the perfect form of revenge.

"I don't need him." These were the words Thuy said a few days before. The guys had been going over a list of couples and matched me with somebody else. She blamed me. It hurt me to hear those words come out of her mouth.

If Thuy didn't need me, then I didn't need her. Saigon's fall had somehow made me tougher, in turn making me seem more attractive, and therefore more popular. Now I could attract girls like Bao Quyen, even if she was not looking for a boyfriend.

"Thanh," my friend Cao said.

I looked at him. Like all of us guys, he smelled like cigarettes and too much cologne.

"She's here," he said.

It was the moment I had been replaying in my mind like a movie scene. I turned around.

Thuy was standing on the corner with friends. The smug smile on my face faded when I gazed at her beauty, her long shiny hair, the way she leaned as she stood.

I got the courage to look at her face. There was sadness in her eyes. I wanted to go to her, to touch her hair. Instead, I looked away and wrapped my hands around my handlebars.

I woke up from my memory. Father Chuong was staring at me tenderly.

"That was the last time you ever saw her?"

I nodded.

"When I knew I was leaving Saigon, I told Bao Quyen. I didn't tell Thuy," I said.

I closed the notebook. More guys poured into the barracks to put their bowls and extra food near their mats.

"And it was a stupid misunderstanding. I never had the chance to say goodbye. I keep seeing those sad eyes."

Talking out loud helped me understand that Thuy would always be the girl I loved.

CHAPTER 44

An Escape

After work on Monday, an alarm echoed through the mountains, a whining circular sound. The guards barked orders until we were all locked inside. So we sat in our cabin for hours. We learned that a guy had escaped.

"He was smart to do it on Sunday. He had all day to run before they missed him at count."

"I thought there was something special about that guy," Tin said.

"You thought he was an antenna," Ms. Dan joked.

"He could have been. He almost made himself invisible," Tin said.

Hoai had been in our barracks. He was older than most of us, in his thirties. He was a tiny guy with a skinny frame and almost bald. He was quiet and unobtrusive. He had no friends in the camp, and no family ever came to visit.

"Turns out he was braver than we thought," Tin said.

I couldn't fathom the idea of escape. It never even occurred to me. There was never a moment when they didn't watch us from the tower. The hillsides were rigged with land mines and many layers of barbed wires. Even if a guy did manage to get past the gates, where would he go? The little village we could see from the hill was a twelve-hour ride from Saigon.

We didn't know exactly what was happening in the world outside the camp, except the Communists were still in control. There would be police and guards wherever Hoai managed to go. He was as emaciated as the rest of us, covered with bug bites and dirt. He'd be spotted easily. His escape was a big mystery.

Two months later, we were gathered together in the yard one afternoon. Guards brought in Hoai. He was wearing civilian clothing—a white button-down shirt and shorts covered in bloodstains. His hands were tied behind his back. His face was swollen badly. He was led past the barracks and to the solitary confinement cell. There was only one for five thousand guys in the camp. To get in, you had to step down then through an iron door.

Most prisoners were left in solitary for a week. Hoai was different. Weeks passed, then months. Some nights I lay awake, imagining all those hours alone in the dark. It took strength to even conceive of escaping. I imagined having to sit with the anguish of that failure.

When they finally let Hoai out, he looked like a starving monkey. His bones poked out of his body. Even his skull showed through. His lips were peeling. He didn't look at us, as if blind. But the worst part was how quiet he got. It was tough for us all to be around him. Even looking at him seemed to hurt Hoai. We wanted to comfort him but didn't know how.

* * *

Tin, Quang, and I sat in our room, devouring watered-down stew made of some dried French broth Tin had gotten from relatives. The sun was starting to lower on the side of the hill.

"Is Hoai okay?"

"Yes. They are letting him go," Ms. Dan said.

Earlier that afternoon, while we were working the fields, a convoy of military jeeps and cars came to K-3. There was some commotion, and two guards hauled Hoai off to headquarters. We all cared about Hoai, even though few actually spoke to him. His deep suffering since then was tough to watch.

"They just wanted a reenactment from him," Ms. Dan said. There were a few guards who liked him for his mild manner and shared the info with him.

"What is that?" Quang asked.

"They wanted him to show them exactly how he did it so they could make sure nobody did it in the future."

I smiled. Hoai had stumped them.

"How? Do you know?" Quang asked.

After my stew was done, I licked my second finger and rubbed it along the bottom of the bowl then licked my finger again. There was nothing left.

Tin was happy I had enjoyed his gift.

"You guys know that trench that rolls down the hill? It starts at the toilet in the back of the camp, where all the shit and dirty water rolls down in the rain," Ms. Dan said.

Quang and I looked at each other and scrunched up our faces. Quang laughed.

"Well, that trench runs along the barbed wire, right?" he continued.

Tin looked up as a guy passed by too closely. We didn't know him.

"Do you guys want to have some tea later on? I have the plants," Ms. Dan asked loudly.

"Sure."

The guy passed by. Ms. Dan waited a few minutes. Then he explained how Hoai had studied the area every Sunday for months. He took note of when the guards' shift changed. Then one Sunday, near the end of his shift, he slid down that trail, amid all the piss and shit. Somehow, he slipped under that barbed wire.

Hoai found himself in a tall grass field. Just past there, the area was loaded with mines. And this guy remembered that if crabgrass or any kind of wildflowers grew, it was unlikely there was a mine there. So he stepped on top of all the thick grass roots without setting anything off. That let him escape.

We were quiet. It was a lot to take in.

Guys in the courtyard were heading back to the barracks.

"How did they catch him?" I whispered.

Ms. Dan took a deep breath.

"Somehow, he made it to Saigon. He didn't go to his family house because the guy is smart. But a little boy, maybe eight years old, recognized him. He asked why he was back in Saigon after being in the camp for five years. Somebody overheard the conversation and reported Hoai. The authorities brought him back."

"He got all the way there." Quang sighed.

I remembered the little kids in our neighborhood the day the Communists took over, the way they tried to block Thinh from going home.

"One guy said they teach kids in school how to report on people," Tin said.

I refused to believe that was what things were like out there.

CHAPTER 45

The Midnight Trains

It had been raining for days. The earth moved imperceptibly, shaking the leaves of the jungle trees, which dripped water into the dry ground. Rain patter trilled from different groups of trees, first behind us then to our right.

The rainy season meant light rain fell on us while we worked, coating our bodies in red mud. When the rains were heavy but expected to be short, the guards made us huddle until it stopped. If it rained for too long, they sent us back to the barracks. The glossy red path wound down Phuong Vi hill like a stream emptying into a river.

I peered into the valley below. Smoke was billowing from a fire. Several women in white shirts were toiling in the cassava field. Nearby was the train station.

"There's supposed to be another train tonight," Quang said.

"Do you think it is true?" I asked.

For about a week, men with higher clearance had been going to the open market at the train station. They heard rumors that thousands of men had been transferred by train.

"I think so. They are probably bringing them to Z-30B."

Z-30B was a mystery to us. It was a labor camp like ours. It was less than a mile away but deep in the jungle. It was a mythological place. The older military men were interned there.

The first camp my father was put in after my mother packed his last lunch was somewhere in the South. That was in 1975, when the Communists won the war. They later transferred him to a camp to the North. He wasn't alone. During those years, they secretly trans-ferred nearly a million formerly high-ranking South Vietnamese offi-cers, scattering them mostly in jungle land in the North. Nobody knew their location.

And they were bringing them back.

"Is it a good sign they are bringing them back? Maybe things are stabilizing?" I asked.

Quang shrugged his jutting shoulders.

I thought about my father, the last time I'd seen him, the sad way he'd looked at me while I smoked the cigarette, the way he thought he had failed me.

I had to believe he'd be on one of those trains.

* * *

The sun pressed on that spot between my bare neck and the ribbon of cloth I had sewn in my shirt. The guys had taught me how to do that to hold it together. We'd gotten a small handful of cassava for lunch. Quang had generously added seeds and salt to my bowl.

It wasn't enough. My stomach was empty. My temples ached. Returning to work after lunch was always the toughest part of the day for me. It always took five minutes of walking before I stopped screaming inside.

"It won't rain again today. The sun is too strong," I said.

"Thanh, don't say that. You will curse us."

I laughed, and that triggered a cough. I took a swig from my Guigoz can, but just a small one since we had hours of work ahead.

"Besides, you are wrong. The wind was moving quickly earlier. There are clouds where the jungle is most dense. They will move in."

"Maybe you are right."

Everyone at camp had become a weatherman. We could pre-dict, by observing how the clouds were traveling, when the rains would start. Even for how long.

Southern rains were our deliverance. They would last at least four hours. The guards would send us back to the barracks. That allowed us to play music, play cards, and cook.

The rain during that season was a rescue from the heavens. It was a benevolent presence that stayed with us, watching, waiting inside the clouds. We prayed directly to it. "Please come. Please come here now."

Occasionally, we heard a loud thunderclap in response.

By 3:00 p.m., my bad mood had eased. Quang had been correct. I hadn't cursed us. We squatted under the trees above the field where we had been working, holding our ponchos over our heads. We huddled close together, ordered so by the guards. Rain made visibility poor, giving prisoners a chance to escape in the past. They were in the forest with waterproof boots and thick rain jackets, glowering at us.

Puddles formed down in the field, thick furrows threatening our delicate corn plants. The corn had grown about as high as our knees. Its roots were well established. But you never knew what would happen. Nobody was meant to live that high in the jungle. You couldn't force nature.

"Slowing down," Tha said.

It wouldn't be a long rain. We'd have to go back to work.

"Too bad," Quang said.

"It's true," Tha came over and whispered. He'd been cursed and hassled by the guards more times than any man in our barracks. But he soon resumed whistling and writing his poems. The rain was still so loud in the canopy of trees, he didn't need to bother to whisper. The guards were well behind us in the middle of the forest, with real waterproof boots and thick rain jackets.

"What's true?"

"The train came in last night. They unloaded thousands of men."

"How do you know?"

"I know. I found out," he said.

I nodded. Tha was probably the guards' least favorite inmate. He was insolent. But he had one friend who was either a guard or a friend of a guard. His information was never wrong.

"Do they know where they came from?"

"North."

"All captains or above? Colonels?"

"Yes. All the old men who managed to stay alive."

The puddles surrounding the plants had stopped rising.

Water pinged off the leaves.

Far behind us, in treetops, something stirred.

"Someone you may know, Thanh?" Tha asked.

I kept my mouth shut.

I believed my father was in that transfer. But I didn't want to jinx it.

The day dried up fast. The sun had returned to draw sweat from our backs before falling below the western horizon. It was 4:00 p.m. We knew that jungle sky so precisely that we put down our tools before the guards told us to.

"Ready to take a bath," Ms. Dan joked.

The rains had been ferocious that year, though, and the ponds had swelled. We ran toward one, ripping our shirts off. When we got there, we took off our rubber tire sandals and put everything up high on the stones beside the well. We looked at the pond.

Two guys were already in there swishing around. Ms. Dan looked at me, smiling, and we jumped in.

When I got in, I couldn't believe how deep the ponds had gotten in the few days since I had been able to bathe. I kept my body straight and my toes pointed and pushed down toward the bottom. They didn't touch, and the water was too muddy to chance going under.

I looked around. Some of the guys were racing each other.

"A hundred yards," I heard one of them say. I looked at Ms. Dan, at Tin.

I flapped around in the pond with my friends. Quang was pushing his arms in great circles. Tha was treading water. I did a stroke to my side and laughed, my mouth filling with dirty water.

To our right was the garden. There was something indecent about it. The vegetables were beautiful. White leafy cabbage, heads of bok choy, light green opo squash, vines of pumpkins about the size of a head. And my favorite, huge Thai basil and mint leaves whose beautiful scent lingered on your fingers if you rubbed it. When the rains came, the scent of piss and shit from the latrine fertilizer made it something acrid.

That didn't stop us from wanting it.

We passed the garden cautiously, our taste for it insatiable. We all held our shirts balled over our bare chests, waiting to see who would snatch something first.

Sometimes, I pretended to slip on the ground and snatched some loot. Otherwise, I rarely picked anything except a handful of mint or basil. The mint was my favorite. It smelled so strong and could make the cassava or dry corn taste like food. I kept walking.

"I'm out," a guy in front of us said. He held some vegetables in his shirt like a baby.

I turned around to see a guard walking behind me, a mean guy with a snarled lip and small eyes who liked to yell and hit people.

Two guys behind him were carrying wood for their fires. They were covered in red mud.

The guard's eyes were like fishhooks that caught me in the chest. There was nothing wrapped in my T-shirt. But the guy didn't need an excuse to hassle me.

I kept my eyes straight ahead. A picture of what I had just seen got lodged in my brain of the guys behind me, still covered in thick red mud. We climbed higher, and our pace picked up.

A strange thought hit me. I remembered the first night I was in K-3 on top of the hill, waiting to be assigned to our barracks. The loud bang of a hammer against the metal railroad track, which marked the end of the workday, startled me. I had looked out the window to see thousands of men in columns, covered in red mud. Men from the train station. I was now one of them.

CHAPTER 46

Unexpected Discovery

They had moved K-3 camp from the hill to a place farther down in the valley. We felt like kings. There was a compound of dozens of long concrete barracks, built out of thick white and gray slabs and square pillars. Of course, there was the barbed wire surrounding it, but there was more room to walk around.

Moonlight spilled through bars on the windows. There were thick concrete floors and wooden platforms for sleeping mats. The best part was there were wells between the barracks for clean water to drink and to bathe in. I poured buckets of clear water over the grime that had collected in every orifice for the last three years of bathing in murky ponds.

The new camp also included some upgrades to our culture and recreation offerings. There was a reading room, dominated by propaganda like the collected works of Lenin. There was a music room where our band could play things that weren't considered yellow music. The visiting room invited traveling relatives to stay overnight. A large courtyard was for soccer team games.

The camp had a real soccer team. A total of twenty-five guys were selected from three thousand inmates to play against the guards. They were assembled twice a year around the holidays to raise morale, or perhaps to give the illusion the camps treated us well. The team members got out of labor work.

The Communist propaganda also declared that the games built friendship between the inmates and guards. But there were hidden

156

risks. Unless the prisoner team threw most of their games, they would suffer a backlash due to the guards' bruised egos.

I stood in front of the barracks, watching people playing soccer in the rain. We had been given the rest of the day off because of the weather. I stood watching skinny guys with mud smeared on their knees and elbows, gritting their teeth as they bounded like rabbits after the ball. I watched the hysterical way they ran. I laughed with them.

Then one guy had the ball, kicking it side to side down the field. He took aim at the makeshift goalposts designated by T-shirts and shoes, aimed, and then shot it past the goalie.

Inspired, I stripped down to my shorts and jumped in barefoot to join the game.

I played soccer as a kid. As I ran up and down the field chasing after the ball, my body remembered every move. I was ecstatic as the mud sucked in my feet.

"Here, over here. I'm open," I said to the guy who had the ball. He used the inside of his foot to pass it to me. I began kicking and coasting down the long field. I was intercepted. I followed the guy who had taken the ball from me then intercepted him and passed it to my teammate, who passed it back. The rain beat down as we were passing the ball back and forth gently, until I finally got where I needed to be. I raised my foot back and shot the ball. I watched the goalie plummet into the mud as the soccer ball went in. The guys on my makeshift team cheered, and I laughed, slapping my hands on my thighs.

After the game, I was toweling the mud off my face with somebody's shirt. Luc, the captain of the camp soccer team, came up. He was a skinny guy with dark skin who spoke with a friendly Southern accent. He was a good player. The captain greeted me.

"I was watching you play. You're good. You should play for the team."

"Oh, really?" I said.

"Yeah."

He was serious. I was tested the next day. I was only better than average, but I made the soccer team!

CHAPTER 47

The Soccer Team

At first, being on the team was exciting. It was nice to be treated specially and have all the privileges. The team practice was hard, but I didn't go home every night with pains shooting down my back every night, like I did with field work. It was so different to be running down a field in the sun chasing after a ball rather than hunched over a machete under the watchful gaze of the guard. But when my friends left for work in the fields, I missed them.

It was not long before the other team members realized I wasn't a great player. I was good enough to be on the bench team. At least in the fields, I knew what I was doing. On the soccer team, I'd never fit in.

One day, we were getting ready to play a scrimmage match with the guards. I was nervous. As the guys started leaving the barracks, I lingered by my bed. The others gathered in front of me. Their comments showed me they were openly skeptical of my abilities as a soccer player.

"You have a game, right?" Quang asked.

Everyone was quiet, waiting for my answer.

"Just a pickup game."

"Well, be careful, Thanh," Tin said. "Keep away from the ball. If you can help it, stay off the field."

The guys all laughed, and I joined them to show I was a good sport.

* * *

I stood on the soccer field with my team for the scrimmage match. I was in the least noticeable position, full back on the right-hand side, but still I stuck out. I played barefoot in the clothes I used to cut corn and cassava while the other guys had full equipment.

And my body wasn't developed. Compared to the other guys, I was puny, having the physique more of a young boy. My legs were getting stronger, but I got dizzy during practice when we did exercises in the hot sun. More than that, I was always hungry.

When we started the pickup game, it was obvious to me that the stakes had changed. Everything about the guards changed. Their bodies were more tense. One made strange chewing motions with his mouth, as if he planned to eat us for dinner.

When the whistle blown and the guard shouted, "Start!" I jumped.

The ball came down the field, and I followed. As much as I would have liked to have taken Tin's advice and stayed away from it, I couldn't do that. I would play as well as I could for my teammates.

Most of the game was a blur. I spent it running back and forth. The dirt cut into my feet, sending shockwaves of pain as far as my ears. As I tried to keep up, the sweat coming out of my pores smelled strange, dirty.

The guards swore loudly. But they didn't exploit their authority. They knew the prisoner team was better than they were since some were professionals before the occupation. They watched us closely to learn some moves.

We stopped and started. Stopped and started. First, we were at one end of the field and then the other. I was trying to keep my feet from getting stepped on by the guards.

The ball came down the field.

Suddenly, a teammate yelled my name. I was open. The guy passed it. But I fumbled, tripping over the ball. It rolled behind me.

A guard swooped around, knocking me to the ground. I watched him, lying on my ass, as he kicked the ball the other way down the field.

CHAPTER 48

The Poem

It was a special night. I wasn't the only one who felt it. We sat on the bench backward, awaiting the teapot to boil, and stared up through the wooden slats on the roof.

Right above us, outside the window, the moon was full. A fat circle of light in the deep blue sky. It was incredible.

"The last time I saw something like that was—" Quang said.

"At the movies," Ms. Dan said, finishing his line.

The moon had released the scents of the jungle, the pungent scent of green fir and juniper bush. A sweetness lingered, maybe from some kind of flower that we never saw.

We only had another hour before they would bang on the steel as a reminder to turn the lights out.

It was my favorite hour.

"Thanh, what's wrong? Does the night sky make you nervous?" the poet asked.

"Ha. No. That's how that guy looks when he's thinking."

I smiled.

The beauty of the night was bittersweet. I couldn't tell anyone about my plan to look for my dad at Z-30B. But I couldn't even trust my closest friends.

"Look at Thanh, smiling so big. He's glowing like that moon. What are you so happy about?"

I opened my mouth to speak.

"Just enjoying the company," I joked.

The guys liked that. They started to laugh.

"Maybe he won a soccer game. Did you finally score a goal?" Ms. Dan joked.

The guys thought that was hilarious, but I didn't mind.

"Of course not. I pulled my thigh muscle though. Think they'll keep me on the bench now," I said.

That started the laughter up more raucously. At least I was still part of the group. They weren't angry with me for being selected.

"Tea's ready," Ms. Dan said. People brought their mugs to the pan, and everyone got a taste.

I approached the pot. Ms. Dan poured some for me.

"It smells great," I said. "What is it?"

"I am not sure," said Ms. Dan. "A friend found it on the hill and gave it to me."

I returned to the bench and took a sip of the tea. It slid down to my heart.

"But I have some news," I blurted out finally. I didn't want to miss my chance.

"What is it?" Tha asked.

"The soccer team, we are going to play an exhibition game in the other camp."

Saying the words made them real. I was going to the other camp.

My father might have been in there.

Somebody whistled like a bird. People were staring at me, trying to take the news in.

Nobody had ever been allowed at Z-30B.

I felt Ms. Dan looking at me.

"What do you think it's like there at Camp B?" somebody said.

"Same as here. How much can they do in the jungle?"

"Don't underestimate."

"Probably fancier. It's for the old guys, so they get the real style. Maybe clean water baths."

Someone laughed, and someone else chattered like a monkey.

"It's the old guys that the Communists are most angry with," someone hissed.

"Amazing if many survived."

Tha sat down beside me. He looked all around, searching for antennas. Then he whispered.

"Tôi bước đi
Không thấy phố,
Không thấy nhà
Chỉ thấy mưa sa
Trên màu cờ đỏ.

I walked alone
There was no town
There was no house
Only rain on the red flag."

He looked at me intensely. "Good poem?"

"Tell me more," I said in the tone we had developed that was as soft and secretive as the language of birds.

"It is about a battle that took place near the old emperor's citadel, during a cold misty rain. The North Vietnamese had captured the site and stuck a red flag in it. It was a forbidden poem by the Communists, written before the war, but it became famous in '72 in the South. Remember that hot summer, near the end of the war, just before Saigon fell?"

I lay on the sandbag pillow stuffed with cotton, the mosquito net already draped over my body. Some guys were already asleep. I felt the vibrations of their steady snoring.

Underneath the planks of my bed was my storage space, where I'd kept the extra loot. In it I used to keep supplies like noodles, real sugar and salt, and containers to store water, including one huge one that could have gotten me thrown into the bunker. There was firewood. Plus my essentials—aluminum bowl, toothbrush, chopsticks, can, two T-shirts, one pants and extra shorts, plus sheet music and letters from my family.

Tha's voice returned in my mind.

Tôi bước đi
Không thấy phố,

Không thấy nhà
I walked alone
There was no town.

I had never heard the poem before. But there was something so striking about it.

Chỉ thấy mưa sa
Trên màu cờ đỏ.
There was no house
Only rain on the red flag.

I remembered that fierce battle Quang Tri in the hot summer of 1972. I thought of the citadel in the mist, a red flag flying from it.

Then I remembered, clearly, that morning I'd stood on the hospital roof, looking at that sea of red flags. How incredible and upsetting they had looked to me then.

It happened five years ago. Five years. Long enough in the past to make those years in Saigon feel like a dream, as if they had never truly existed.

Again, I remembered my father at the door with his lunch packed, the sad look in his eyes.

"Do you know anyone who may be there in Camp B?" Tha asked.

I liked Tha for the same reason everyone did. He had the courage to say what he wanted. It was more than brave of him to recite the poem in the barracks. At first, he hadn't seemed like himself. But then he was his old self, reciting yellow poetry in the barracks. Was he growing bolder because he had somehow given up?

I lay there in my bed with my eyes open. I tried to bring back my father's face, his wide forehead, his deep laughing eyes. I tried to plan what I would do once I got to the game. Would I be able to sneak away and go find him? Ask around and find out if he was still alive?

Compared to Tha and most of the other guys, I considered myself to be weak, a guy just floating along. It was true I was too young to have the chance to fight like they had after the war had ended. And in all those years of captivity, my courage had never really been tested.

I was half asleep when the guard banged the gong at 10:00 p.m. My eyelids fluttered open again.

Someone stood up to blow out the lamp. Just then, I heard someone stumbling out from the corner of the room. Hong emerged from a big cloud of smoke from the front of the room, a skinny guy with a narrow face and a slight hunchback. He made his way to the front of the room. His nightly routine. He wheezed like a kid faking a heart attack. His wheezing was like an old radiator hissing. Someone cursed at him. Someone else laughed. He wheezed and fell down on the floor. He lay there, breathing really hard, but we had grown tired of his jokes, so Hong made his way to bed. He made one final gesture, slamming himself down on the bed. *Whoomppph.*

I laughed quietly.

Then the guy in the front blew out the light.

CHAPTER 49

Where Are You, Dad?

I had to force myself to stay on the bench during the game at Camp B. I scanned the field looking for evidence of my father, using the photo of him in my mind. I realized he would have aged since we last saw each other, but maybe not that much. Okay, his hair might have changed, his hair that was always meticulously cut to regulation length with a close-cropped buzz in the far back by his neck. Nobody could keep their hair groomed in the camps. So it wouldn't be neat anymore. There might even be a little gray.

The game was underway. It was a nice grass soccer field a bit smaller than ours.

I couldn't keep my eye on the game, though. I promised myself I would stay ten minutes.

My relationship with my dad might have been distant when I was growing up, but I'd gotten to know him better in those last days. Besides, we were family. We were blood. I would know him, sense him, if he was around.

Since it was an exhibition game, all the inmates from Camp B were allowed to come out and watch. They stood in great groups around the field. I scanned the field and looked at every older man's face.

I looked toward another group. The guys pressed together looked more sickly, more damaged than we were. My father wasn't in that sad group.

I decided to watch the game for a while.

When I had the opportunity, I slipped behind the bench, then behind a crowd of men, and then another crowd, blending until I was able to make my way to the barracks.

I was taking a chance. I didn't know these guards. I didn't know what they did to people who disobeyed Camp B rules.

I stopped at the end of the field near two old men, slightly hunched into each other as if having a secret conversation. They appeared to be squinting at the wind, slight smiles on their faces, like old men who were old enough to act like children again. I decided they were safe, that they weren't antennas.

"Excuse me, Uncles. I am looking for my father."

"What?" one yelled, practically spitting at me.

I'd picked the wrong ones.

"I'm looking for my father," I repeated.

Nobody else, thankfully, was paying any attention.

"Who is your father?"

"He is Nguyễn Văn Toàn."

The old man looked up, like he was staring at an invisible bird in the sky.

"Maybe I know him. What was his rank?" the other guy asked.

"Lieutenant colonel."

The crowd roared. Somebody had scored a goal. The old men turned to look at the field.

I waited. I tried to be patient. I only had a few more minutes before they noticed I was gone.

"Please, Uncles. My father was a lieutenant colonel. I think he may have come in on the last train from the North. Um, the train three nights ago."

The first man nodded, a long slow nod.

"Maybe. Maybe you will find him somewhere near the barracks."

"Do you know him?"

"Maybe you will find him near the barracks," he repeated.

"Or if you see a fat old man near there, his name is An. You ask him. He knows everyone who came in on the train."

"Where are the barracks?"

He looked over my head then down at me again. "You are from Camp A?"

I nodded.

"Behind the crowd, to the right, there is a path. The barracks are about one quarter kilometer up the hill. It's empty now since most are down here. But be careful."

* * *

The major difference between Camp B and ours was that there were a lot more trees and shrubs around, and the bugs were ferocious. The concrete barracks were set up in a similar configuration to ours.

Eventually, I came to a clearing where some guys closer to Quang's age were standing, and others were sitting on logs. They were surprised to see me.

I stood in front of them, feeling vulnerable, hoping there was guard behind me, waiting to slam me onto the ground.

"Excuse me. I am looking for—"

The guys were staring up at me.

"My uncle and my father. They may have been brought in recently from the North. My dad is Nguyễn Văn Toàn. My uncle is Nguyễn Văn Hoà. Does anyone know them?"

The older man looked like he was trying to remember. I bent over to look him in the eyes. They were milky, the way old men's eyes get when they have a cataract, or they have seen too much.

"What is your name?"

"Thanh."

"How did you get here?"

"Please, Uncle. I haven't seen him since he left home five years ago."

The old man studied me for a second. He placed a twig in his mouth and began sucking.

"I am sorry. I don't know him."

By the time I got to the other row of barracks, my calves were aching. All that soccer hadn't made them stronger. The camp was about twenty times the size of our camp.

I gave myself another ten minutes to explore each area.

When I started to feel discouraged, I thought of my uncle visiting us after solitary with a smile on his face, looking at the mountains and writing a poem.

I visualized my dad, but I imagined the man with the cataract. I imagined finding him and myself hugging him, something we'd never done in my home.

I felt oddly responsible for him being in this place, for his aging, for what I was sure was the deterioration of his mind. I felt that finding him would make him get better.

I stopped at a clearing farther in the camp. It was quiet. The ground was blanketed with needles.

I was so tired. I thought briefly how nice it would be to lay down on those needles and go to sleep. I noticed a solitary man with his back against a tree. He was the only one there.

Slowly, I walked over to him. When I spoke, his eyes looked startled.

"Hello, Uncle."

He looked at me strangely. I wondered if he was deranged.

"I don't mean to bother you."

"No bother," he said. He smiled slightly, as if touched at the sentiment.

"Tell me, Uncle. Have you been in this camp for a while?"

He squeezed his eyes shut and then opened them.

"Maybe four years."

"Are you from Saigo—"

"Saigon," he repeated. He tilted his chin up.

"Where do the men in this camp come from?"

"There are many men here. Three thousand live here."

His eyes still looked startled. I wondered if they were always that way.

"But who are the men? Do they all come from the same place?"

"No. All over. From different camps, mostly in the North. Why? Who are you?" he asked.

"I am trying to find my father, Nguyễn Văn Toàn. I thought he might be in this camp."

He looked at me then, his eyes softened.

"I'm sorry, son. I don't know him."

"Does anyone know him? Can you find out? Please. I don't have much time left."

He looked at me, the startled look back in his eyes.

"You must go back, son. It is not safe."

I had returned to the bench for the end of the second half of the game. I had slipped back, like nothing had happened. I sat on the end of the bench, completely winded, panting.

A teammate who I had confided in looked at me, his eyes expectant.

I shook my head. His eyes filled with sympathy, then he looked back toward the game.

I sat there staring at the teams. A sadness engulfed me. I hadn't felt that way in a while.

I hadn't felt anything.

* * *

The dull hum of anger screeched inside like the death rattle of a bird.

I recalled the sound of my dad's music that morning I'd jumped on his belly. Perhaps it really was not the sound but the vibration of it, the way I could feel it in every nerve, even from the other room. I remembered once more, like a knife in my heart, how my father looked at me smoking the cigarette in the living room, the day that he left the house with his lunch.

It wasn't fair, I thought.

I thought of the old men with their startled rheumy eyes, heads cocked toward the sky.

Who are you? they had asked. *How did you get here?*

How had it happened? How had they snatched up so much of our lives?

CHAPTER 50

Hopeless

It was dinnertime. Some of us guys were outside, cooking over small fires, savoring the free time. Our makeshift stove was artillery steel balanced over the wood flame. Quang was cooking dried shrimps his family had brought. He stirred in beans, trying to make a stew.

Two guys came from the kitchen, putting a handful of dry corn and a ladle of saltwater into each bowl. Quang added to the pot a pinch of obo squash and a small bit of dried papaya.

It was a lot of food.

"I told you it would rain," Quang said.

"I guess you were right," I said.

Quang shook the pan a little, making sure the dried shrimps didn't burn.

"You want your corn hot?" he asked.

"No. We can just pour the stew on top."

"I think so too," Quang said.

I tried not to stare at Quang while he worked. I didn't want to appear greedy. I'd been eating alone without him for a few months. Quang and I shared the food from our family's visit. But I no longer had much to contribute. My family could no longer visit me. But Quang was kind enough to ask me to join him when he had something special.

I walked back into the barracks, where some guys were already eating. Some guys were using fingers for spoons. Nobody was speaking much. At mealtime, guys were reverent.

A skinny short man named Du picked at his bowl of corn and water in a dignified manner. He was poor but wouldn't accept anyone's food.

Behind him was a sloppy man, acting like a dog waiting for something to drop. He always scarfed his food down, barely taking the trouble to swallow. Nobody liked this man. People suspected that he was an antenna. His bed was the closest to the latrine.

Quang came in with a hot pot he held with a T-shirt. He set the pot down.

I lifted his bowl to him first.

"No, put them both on the ground. It is too hot."

Quang held the can over the bowls and poured equal amounts. He didn't spill a drop.

He nodded at me, a slight smile on his face. We picked up chopsticks and started to eat.

Men slurped quietly from their bowls.

In a few minutes, it would be 6:00 p.m. and they would lock us in the barracks.

CHAPTER 51

The Unthinkable

February 1981

The whole camp sat in groups on the floor in the new large wooden hall. They were facing the stage and the loudspeakers, waiting for the chief police officer to get up on the stage.

He was ready to give a blustery speech filled with propaganda about what was happening outside and how society was banding together, adapting to the new regime.

The loudspeaker kicked in abruptly. Everyone quieted down, watching the officer already standing on stage. There would be consequences if we didn't listen to the program.

"Attention. Attention. You must maintain order and decorum. If you do not listen to the officers, there will be consequences. There is some news."

Some guys fidgeted. It was still early.

"There is going to be a release from the camp. The following individuals will be released from K-3 Reeducation Camp. Nguyen van A, April 24, 1950, Danang. Tran van B, June 3, 1954, Thua Thien. Pham phu A, Jan 4, 1951, Saigon."

There was a long awkward pause, a kind of collective disbelief about what the officer was saying. In the past, every so often, an officer would come to a barracks, excuse a guy or two from labor work, and later we'd find out they'd been released. It was uncommon though, and as more names were read, we began to sense the enormity of what was happening.

As the list of names started growing, guys started cheering. Some stood up wildly, congratulating the ones whose names had been called. Some were crying or laughing. Most of us were in some phase of shock. There were no sentences at K-3. Some of the guys had been there even before the end of the war, nearly eight years before. At some point, most of us had given up hope of ever leaving the camp.

The names kept coming and were greeted by cheers from the crowd. Slowly, I came to understand what was actually happening. They didn't seem to be called in any particular order. After all, all kinds of guys had been sent to the camp—men who had tried to flee the country, resistance members, ex-officers for the South in the Army or Navy.

This went on for hours. The room started getting really loud, and I stood up at about the same time I heard the roar behind me. It occurred to me the last name that was called was Tin, and the next one was the poet. A few hours later, they started calling the names of some of the guys who had been with me in the South.

"Vuong Que Phu, October 29, 1959. Nguyen Xuan Hong, April 2, 1960."

I rushed over to my friends and loudly started congratulating them, my knees turning watery, my head light like when I didn't get enough food. Noise rushed my ears, a persistent white noise. It took me a second to realize it was a hum in the loudspeaker.

I thought I might be in that group. I kept waiting to hear my name.

I saw it all as if in slow motion. I was aware that mostly everyone was standing up, their limbs all unruly despite the largeness of the room. Some officers who had been standing outside came in, just as shocked as we were by what was happening. Then they regained their composure and started yelling, "Stay with your groups" and threatening discipline.

I saw the unadulterated joy in my friend Tin's face and in Quang's face. They still had not yet called my name, but there was a joy surging in my chest, so powerful it almost hurt me.

The next thing I knew, two of the officers had grabbed me. Each had me by one arm and were practically carrying me through the room and out the door. My feet were no longer touching the ground.

They locked me in the library next to the first aid station. I looked through the wooden slats. I could still see the hall a hundred meters away, still hear the loudspeaker reading the names. Occasionally, I saw the guards dragging another unruly few guys from the hall, locking them in different places.

It didn't occur to me that they wouldn't call my name, that I would be stuck in the camp. But the joy that I felt was still uncontainable. I kept walking back and forth, back and forth, pacing around the tiny room as the names continued, like a song with new verses.

Then I heard my name called, and then my birth year. I stopped pacing, and joy surged inside me. I took off my straw hat and threw it so hard up in the air that I hurt my arm. I screamed out in pain, but I was too happy for it to hurt much.

I thought I would cry, but I didn't. I realized it was because after all those years, there were no tears left in me.

CHAPTER 52

The Journey Home

We walked down the hill silently, as if walking through a heavy fog. I was wearing my cleanest labor camp shirt. I had mended one small tear by using the backstitch that Ms. Dan had taught me. The shirt had the K-3 *trại học tập cải tạo* (reeducation camp) stamp on the back, matched by my cleanest pants. I was carrying a small bag with a pair of military pants as a souvenir, a small amount of money they had given us to get back home, and the official document that authorized us to walk outside as free men.

"Don't look back. It's a curse," guys were whispering. I obeyed them, walking somewhere in between quick and slow, carefully, as we stepped down to the area where we hadn't been since arriving at K-3.

When we finally got to the long wooden gate, we stopped. It was already open. We walked through without incident. I took a few steps away from the hundreds of guys around me who were stumbling past the gate, some of whom had sped up and were practically running as their lungs filled with the free air. Once I was sure the area where I was standing was clear and I wouldn't get mauled by any of the guys moving through the gate, I stopped and did something taboo. I turned around.

I wanted to take a mental picture of the camp for the last time, to keep that last image in my memory so I would remember it for as long as I lived.

I looked at the twenty-foot-tall wooden fence and gate, barbed wire wound in circular patterns up its side.

It was around ten in the morning. The sun was already warm on my back. Everyone left in the camp was out in the fields working.

The camp looked so much smaller from the distance, only a few hundred yards.

There was smoke coming out of the big kitchen. I looked toward the big court where I'd played soccer. It was empty. A few cleaners were working along its edge.

I stared at the barracks which had been my home. A few guys were left in there. To the far right was the first aid station, the woodshed, and the little library where I had stood pacing. Just behind that was the gigantic main hall where we'd often sat on the floor, being forced to listen to propaganda, and where we learned we were free men.

I thought of the kitchen with all the smoke coming out. K-3. That was the place I had been all those months, squatting in the barracks late at night under the oil lamp, drinking strange boiled teas and listening to the guys tell their stories. I thought of playing soccer, hunched over the cornstalks which I sliced through with my machete while the sweat covered my body. This was the place where I thought I would die.

But now I was leaving.

I looked toward the mountain, which I'd been staring at for so many years. It appeared larger closer up, no longer part of a dream. Everything looked differently: the roads, the large open space, the vast fields where farmers cared for corn and cassava.

As we got closer to the train station, I saw the village, that place that had been so far away it had barely existed. It was the place where ordinary life had taken on an almost mystical quality in our minds, so much so that it was like we were entering heaven.

The town merchants greeted us with intense kindness, congratulating us as if we were relatives coming home. For years, they had known we were up there, suffering behind the barbed wire. They were Southerners, on the same political side as us, and many of them had relatives who had been sent to camps like that one. The people around us were so happy for us, they were pouring their hearts to us. At first, I didn't understand why. It then occurred to me that there was a rebelliousness in it, as they all had been forbidden to talk to us for so long.

We were walking along the main street of town so casually it seemed like a mistake. We walked past the open-air market and the row of stores. I watched as many of the guys were stopped as towns-people asked them questions.

"Congratulations, nephew," a merchant told me.

I opened my mouth to speak, but nothing came out.

"Would you like a drink? Sugarcane juice," he said and shoved a pouch at me.

I held it in my hand, marveling at the heavy ice cubes at the bottom. I hadn't seen ice cubes since I was captured.

"Where is your family?" he asked.

"Saigon," I said.

"Saigon! Saigon!" he started shouting to people gathered around his shop, gesturing at me. "It is far. Maybe 150 miles. All day on the bus," he explained.

I nodded. Those numbers meant nothing to me. I took a sip of the sugarcane juice. The concentrated sweetness made my throat tighten, and I coughed in surprise. It was delicious.

"All day on the bus," he repeated.

"That's okay," I managed.

"Do you have enough money?"

"Yes, thank you," I said.

"Would you like some sticky rice?"

"No. Thank you." I patted my stomach.

I was not sure how I floated past the man on the street, but I moved with the crowd of confused guys in shirts like mine, moving as one body, occasionally tripping. It's as if like someone was herding us, guiding us through the tiny clogged streets of the town toward the bus station. There I bought a ticket and climbed on board.

They crammed us on a bunch of busses among ordinary people traveling to Saigon. I stared out the window at all the guys in outfits like mine, who still appeared dirty and lost despite all the shaving and showering and combing that morning to make ourselves look presentable. I stared at the other people, mostly farmers, men with

FRANK THANH NGUYEN

strong and wiry bodies, the women with their hair pulled back in buns, some wearing the same black shirts and pants as my mother did the time she visited me in the jail. It was strange to see so many women, and even stranger to see children with them.

I was sitting by the window and pressed my forehead against the glass then let my head fall back on the seat rest. It was quiet on the bus, each of us lost in our own thoughts. I tried to imagine what I would find in Saigon. It was likely my eldest brother was the only one left. I worried that our old house would be taken over by Communists.

We were suddenly moving. The bus was rolling down the dirt road, and the village was getting smaller. Then the bus stopped abruptly.

There were people wearing camp uniforms, former prisoners like me, walking down the road. The driver opened the front door, gestured wildly for them to get on board. But they shook their heads no, politely declining the ride.

There were hundreds of them. I didn't know what they were planning on doing. Maybe they would hitchhike, but I knew in my heart some would walk all the way to Saigon.

As we pulled past them, I couldn't make out many of their expressions, but I could see by the animated movement of their steps they were happy. They were finally able to make their own decisions again. They wanted to walk and feel the joy of their freedom in every step.

I turned toward the window and watched them on the side of the road as the bus rolled faster and they got farther and farther away.

178

CHAPTER 53

Home

It was late at night by the time the bus arrived in Saigon. Walking through the bus station, past small groups, I was acutely aware of how I must have appeared, the stench of my body after sweating on the bus for eight hours.

It was a strange sensation to be alone for the first time in four years, after being always surrounded by guards or fellow prisoners. In the camp, life may have been hard, but no matter what happened, I was never alone. In four years, I hadn't felt lonely.

As I hurried out onto the street, the loneliness worsened like an ache in my belly. Saigon was different from what I remembered after the war had ended. The streets were dark, but there were people out. They were bolder, laughing and shouting. Dozens of motorbikes passed.

The streets seemed strange to me, unrecognizable, although I vaguely knew where I was. I decided to go to my aunt's house. She lived alone in an apartment nearby. I hoped I could find it.

What I remember the most from that first night of freedom was the long cold shower I took in the tiny bathroom in my aunt's tiny apartment in Saigon. I stood there under the stream of water, pounding my shoulders and back. I felt the bar of soap slip over my arms and belly.

My aunt screamed with surprise when I told her who it was through the apartment door. I was shocked by the sadness that had gathered on her face in the years that she had been alone—after my uncle had been taken to a labor camp and her daughter escaped to New Zealand. The small apartment where she had set up the bed for me seemed forlorn.

I shut off the shower quietly and used the towel she gave me. Then I stepped into my uncle's clean pajamas. I sat down on the toilet to collect myself, to think about where I might wind up the next day. My aunt thought my brother was still in Saigon. Beyond that, she didn't know much.

I reached my family's house just after nightfall the next day. It was not taken over by Communists. There were tenants who had rented out most of our family's house. They had to go to find my brother at his girlfriend's house and tell him I was back. The tenants all knew my story and treated my return in a celebratory manner. They were polite and tried to give me my privacy. I heard them whispering and saw the way they glanced when they walked past me toward the kitchen.

I waited for my brother to return.

"Thanh!" he screamed out from the street.

He unlocked the door. I looked at him. His expression was calm, his hair still slightly too long. He didn't appear any differently than he had when we were kids, the carefree older brother who listened to rock and roll albums while we took our naps.

He walked over to me slowly. Then he hugged me. It was a strange gesture for our family, even when times had been good. It was a strange intimacy for any Vietnamese family. He hugged me so tightly, long enough that I didn't have any choice but to relax into it.

"It's perfect. It's perfect," he kept repeating.

He brought me to one of two rooms that weren't rented out. I sat awkwardly on my new bed, and he looked closely at me from a chair near the dresser. The room was barely lit by one dim lamp on the desk.

"Are you feeling okay? Your health, I mean? Is it okay?"

I nodded and tried to smile. I looked at my cracked laborer's hands in my lap.

"I'm going to sleep at No's house tonight. It will give you time to get adjusted. Okay?"

"Yes," I said. I ran my fingers against the blanket on the bed. It felt rough, overwashed. "How is she?"

"She is my girlfriend. No, my fiancé. We are getting married next month. It is perfect you are back now. It was my deepest wish that you and Father would be at the wedding. Well, one of you will."

"Congratulations," I said and tried to smile.

Marriage. Fiancé. Wedding. Those were just words. None of it made any sense.

"Father?" I asked.

"Still in the camp."

I nodded and dragged my fingers across the blanket.

"It will end soon. Someday. It has to," my brother said.

I looked at my brother, noticed the way his face creased, briefly, in disgust. The expression passed though. He still looked like a rebellious teenager, the one that nothing bad could ever touch. It was comforting to see him this way, although of course I couldn't tell if the expression was real or my memory. I didn't know that my brother was even real.

He brushed his long hair out of his eyes in his usual playboy manner.

"I waited. That's why I stayed. In case you returned. Or Father."

"Thanks," I said.

He looked at me seriously, as if there was something he wanted to say. But his expression changed, as if he felt sorry for me and had thought better of it.

"You look exhausted. You probably didn't sleep much there," he said.

I didn't know if he meant at my aunt's house or the labor camp.

"I am a little tired. It is just very different back here. A lot to return to."

"I still have the boat," he said.

"The boat?"

"Didn't you know it? Mother got it for us. It is an old boat, but that's the only way you can manage it now. The authorities will never give a new boat a permit."

There were footsteps in the hallway, the sound of the tenants walking and laughing, bowls being set on the table.

"It is old but has good bones. I have been working on it for the past two years. I'll show it to you soon. By spring, she should be ready," he said.

"Ready for what?" I said.

He looked at me as if I was stupid.

"Thanh, the boat from Mom is our last hope. We cannot stay here."

CHAPTER 54

Reentry

Saigon had sickened. Streets were practically filled with coffee stalls. I saw the pinched faces of strangers. There were women with children in tow, women hunched over wood tables lined with Communist newspapers and splitting coconuts, street sweepers hosing down sidewalks. There was a desperate nervousness as the people moved like birds pecking the ground before a long rain. Otherwise, their business seemed like a theatrical performance to me, masks they put on to adjust to the new regime.

People kept their distance, as if they could sense a sickness on me. They looked toward me but never at me.

Things seemed surreal. All the food we had fantasized while stuck in the barracks was suddenly there, in front of my face on vendor carts. Thant sticks of meat roasted, the fatty scent filling the air. Pots full of rice and grain. Steam drifting off cups and bowls. Instead of tempting me, it disgusted me. When I got to take a bite or a sip or a spoonful of something, it tasted metallic or soapy. More often than not, eating made me sick. It was as if everything was laced with poison.

Everywhere I walked, I imagined that I saw men from the camps. Not only Quang and Ms. Dan and Tha and Tin but the hundreds whose names I never knew, the ones still in jails and the camps. Even the ones who had died of sickness or been shot point-blank.

Everywhere I walked, I saw blood.

How dare I walk free while they were still suffering? How dare I walk wherever I choose, use the toilet alone, eat real rice?

Somewhere in the netherworld—in between what I tried to believe and what I feared—was my father. It was difficult to think about him for too long. I kept my head and shoulders down because every time I looked too closely at anyone else, I suspected they had been conditioned to report me.

The longer I walked, the less safe I felt. A few Communist officials were still walking around in their fancy green suits with the emblems on their chest, but they didn't do any of the dirty work themselves. Mainly they were puffed up with false pride, fixated only on preventing anyone from challenging their authority.

I put my palm on my chest every so often, pressing in. It was an unconscious habit I'd developed, I guess to remind myself I was alive.

The roar of voices assaulted me as soon as we stepped into the coffee shop. They were loud enough to drown out the rock and roll music.

There were so many different people in there, sitting at tiny tables that spilled onto the sidewalk. They were kids who had family abroad and were rich enough to turn themselves into hippies. Girls with long unbrushed hair and wide-legged foreign jeans. Playboys in ironed dress shirts, smoking cigarettes imported from Thailand. Guys wearing leather who traded on the black market. Even some wealthy Chinese.

My friends pushed me through the crowd, giving me a tour.

"You see where the DJ sits, Thanh? He is Chieu, Bao Quyen's brother. You know them, right? You see all those records?" Cao said. Even though he was a little heavier than the rest of us, girls liked him because he was charismatic, an extrovert who had no problems speaking his mind. He could be generous but was a bit of a trickster. Everyone teased him about the way he brazenly lied.

He was annoying me by pushing me closer to the DJ booth at the far corner of the café. I could see a few of the records—the Bee Gees, Boney M, some disco.

We stood close to two huge loudspeakers. The music was so loud it echoed through me.

"Let's sit down," Minh said. Of the two of them, I was closer to Minh. He was a quiet guy and one of my few friends who I really trusted because he knew how to listen. He made you feel he could understand anything you were saying. If I would have opened up to anyone, it would have been him. But I couldn't. I realized that I didn't feel connected to my old friends. Only a few left. Too much had happened to change me.

We found a table far enough away from the music where we could be heard.

Thu smiled gently at me. She was very pretty, with her heart-shaped face and hair falling to her shoulder. She'd always been more mature than the other girls, aware of how to use her beauty. In the four years that had passed, she'd turned into a woman. It was difficult to look at her.

Cao made his way back through the outdoor café, greeting people at every table he passed. He brought two cups of coffee back to our table, setting one in front of me.

"Welcome back," Minh said.

I nodded. I took a sip of the coffee. It was so strong and gritty I had to be careful to control my expression. My senses were overwhelmed.

The day dragged on. Minh and Cao both drifted around from table to table like hummingbirds drawn to flowers. Minh was still skinny and awkward. He still walked funny.

"So what was it like?" Minh asked me.

"What?"

"The labor camp."

"Not too bad."

"Well, you must have worked hard. Look at those muscles. Look at how buff you are! Bet you could beat me now," Cao said.

"Your arms are so big," Thu said.

"Yeah, looks like a good way to get fit," Minh said. "Go to the labor camp. How did they catch you again?"

I took another sip of the coffee. Every time I opened my mouth, I was unsure if anything would come out. Everyone was silent, waiting for me to respond.

"It's a long story. We thought they were the resistance. It was a trap."

They stared at me, waiting for more. I didn't have anything left to give. Like most teenage boys in Saigon, both of my old friends had tried to escape and gotten caught. They stayed in a camp for a few weeks, found a way to buy their freedom, and then came back to the city. It was like a game. I was the only one labeled a political prisoner, a real threat to the Communists. That was the reason they held me so long.

"And so tan," someone exclaimed.

"He's skinny though. You didn't get much good food," Cao joked.

"We ate," I said, ashamed of how defensive the words sounded. "Excuse me," I said. I stood up and pretended to go to the bathroom on the other side of the café. When I got far enough away, I stood against the wall and looked back toward the table. Cao was gesturing wildly, probably telling a story about someone. Thu was making a funny face and waving her hand in front of her nose to say that it was not true. Minh was just sitting there, wearing a thin smile.

Quietly, I made my way out of the café and onto the street.

I stood on the street, trying not to stare at the people at the dingy outdoor tables. The noise was less intense there, but it was uncomfortable to be around strangers. I was now in typical teenager clothes—my one pair of Levi's and a pressed shirt, the top two buttons undone. My long hair was stylish. Still, I felt anyone could identify me as a former labor camp prisoner. The years I'd spent away had turned me into a freak.

The weirdest part about being home was all the freedom. Nothing was scheduled anymore. Although we still had to be careful, I was allowed to walk anywhere I wanted. It could feel nice, walking up and down paved streets. But it could also be overwhelming.

"Thanh," I heard a woman's voice say. It was Thu, standing there with her long legs in a short miniskirt. She ran over to me, cocked her head, and smiled.

"You aren't a Boney M. fan?" she joked.

I just shook my head. The city had changed so much since I was gone. "No. I like that song."

She waited. Thu was one of the four girls who hung out with Thuy. She was always the giddiest, the loudest, but she loved Thuy dearly. She was still attractive, though it was strange to see her all grown up.

"I don't know. It was just a little loud in there. So much commotion."

She opened her purse and pulled out some expensive cigarettes. She offered me one and lit it. I inhaled. The smoke brought back pleasant memories.

"I understand," she said.

I nodded. But I knew that she didn't.

"Do you care if I stay out here a little?" she said. "Cao is annoying me."

I laughed. I looked at the café. In the street, dozens of motorbikes were parked.

"There are more bikes now than before. There is a lot more of everything."

"Like what?"

"I don't know. Blue Jeans. Vinyl."

"I knew you didn't like the music."

"Stop. I like it. I actually like it a lot."

She looked around quickly then stood closer and spoke quietly.

"They open the border up every few months or so. Then everyone abroad sends things—money, blue jeans, vinyl. They do it just long enough. So when they close it, there are more riches in there. Sometimes it gets confiscated. But mostly it circulates and makes everyone richer."

She suggested we walk a little.

I nodded.

We walked slowly, silently.

"Thuy really cared for you," she said.

I nodded.

"She got your letter."

I took another drag of the cigarette.

"The one you threw from the bus. The street sweepers delivered it to her house."

I got a head rush. It was a nice feeling.

"When she heard that they took you, she cried hard. She was inconsolable. I think that was a big reason why."

"Why?" I asked.

"Why she withdrew so much before you left? I knew that she liked you, Thanh, but I didn't know how much."

Something inside me snapped. I felt the tears in my throat. I looked away.

"I have to go see my brother," I said, more abruptly than I had intended.

I felt her looking at me. I didn't want to be an object of pity.

Gently, she touched my shoulder.

"Thanh, can we get some coffee another time? I have something to give you."

I nodded, afraid I would cry if I tried to speak.

CHAPTER 55

The Boat

I lay on my bed in my room and waited. My muscled body now felt useless, and I was sure the rich foods, still foreign to me, were making me lazy.

My brother Thach came into my room and surprised me. He was usually not at home.

"You want to go see the boat later this week?" he asked.

"Okay," I said, not wanting to seem too anxious.

I invited him out for coffee or lunch. But Thach told me he was going to see his wife.

I didn't respond. I didn't expect Thach to take care of me, but I would have liked it if he'd shown more concern since my return. He'd only come to visit me once at the labor camp, after my mom had escaped, and even then he'd seemed uninterested. Did he care about anything I'd been through the past four years? Or had he gotten too spoiled living in Saigon all these years, unscathed, living the same smooth life he had when we were kids?

I stretched out my legs on the bed, aware that my presence was making Thach uncomfortable, that he wanted to leave the room.

Maybe he avoided me because he could see what I could when I looked in the mirror. He knew that part was still missing, wandering around in his own filth in the sugarcane fields. Maybe he could also sense that his little brother had turned into a ghost.

My brother and I traveled by scooter alongside the places where the Saigon River split into smaller channels before spilling out into the ocean. The deeper we traveled, the more foreign the terrain seemed to me as we slipped past the suburbs and through Chinatown, where a network of canals crisscrossed the city. We went over the Y bridge, where three prongs extended to different neighborhoods.

The deeper we traveled, the poorer the neighborhoods got. The canals clogged, and mosquitoes and gnats that gathered around the still water viciously bit our cheeks and necks.

My brother knew every curve as we careened through tight alleys until we reached District Four, renowned for violent gangs pushing opium. People walked aimlessly there, as if detached from their bodies. The stench of urine and rotting trash emanated.

This area was as foreign to me, as the South had been. It was disordered in a way that the city never was since the Communists took over, and I felt there was a different kind of violent hierarchy which had existed. It was a place where the people in power likely paid off the authorities. It was attractive to me for this reason. But I had to open my mouth to breathe in the heavy stench-filled air.

The streets widened, and we traveled farther from the city. We crossed an old steel bridge built by the French during World War II and passed over a small lagoon. We reached a small island, like a sandbar. Guys stood on the dock, building boats. We coasted over a few small twisted and crooked dirt roads until we got to a house on the riverbank. There were dozens of small fishing boats anchored there, bobbing alone in the water. We parked in a lush green area, shaded by palm trees.

As we walked toward the house where some guys stood on the deck and others on the dock working on the construction, I started to feel strange. There were too many people.

My brother and I waited in the strange house on the island. Men were talking loudly and drinking beer. Some were napping on cots.

The men's drunken voices in the middle of the afternoon disoriented me. We were in a land that was disordered in a way that was rare since the Communists took over. It was a place where the people in power likely paid off the authorities, where an ancient brand of justice ran like an undercurrent of electricity.

The big boss arrived and sat across from us. He was in his forties and had red cheeks. The expression on his face reflected the boredom that comes from living a life of pampered recreation—a quality I'd only noticed in gangsters and the very wealthy, like Tám Điệu and Kha. The dock owner's daughter hovered around the boss. She had mischievous almond-shaped eyes and was around my own age. I kept my eyes on the table's edge.

It was awkward to encounter pretty girls. I'd returned from the labor camp a grown man, still skinny but buff, my muscles developed from years of digging into the rocky earth and slashing through cornstalks. Women now noticed me in a new way that made my body flood with desire so intense it bordered on pain. I avoided them when I could because I was unsure how to respond.

I didn't know how to respond to men either. I believed the camp was still on me, clinging to my skin like a film. I sipped a beer at the table and felt lost, insignificant. There were guys slapping cards on the table, laughing and talking so quickly I couldn't keep up.

"Hi, boss," my brother eventually said.

The guy looked up. He nodded, but it was almost as if my brother's existence was of no consequence. Then he smiled enthusiastically, but his smile remained plastered on his face.

"Thanh, this is Big Brother Hùng," my brother said.

I nodded respectfully, keeping my gaze from his eyes. He continued to smile then turned back to the game.

On the bank just before the monkey bridge, I saw our boat, which my brother dragged all the way from the coast a hundred kilometers away to here several years ago. He tore it apart and rebuilt it. It was fifteen meters long and painted gray, the stern tilted high in the air like it was ready to launch into the ocean but wedged against the muddy bank under the monkey bridge.

The most solid part about the boat was in its age. It was already registered. People could no longer build brand-new boats and register them because that would raise suspicion of escape. I understood the hard work my brother had invested, but it was hard to imagine how this shaky vessel could be seaworthy enough to survive weeks of hard travel on the ocean. It saddened me that this tiny boat was our last shot at freedom.

"Come on, Thanh," my brother said and started running toward the monkey bridge. I slowly followed.

The monkey bridge was a handmade wood bridge nailed together which stood about one meter above the muddy bank. The tide was low, so the monkey bridge was fully extended, and we had to run fifteen yards to get there.

Even though the drop down wouldn't be so bad, and the worst thing that could happen would be that we'd drop down into the mud, I was suddenly scared. There were no handrails. Crossing the monkey bridge suddenly seemed riskier than all the things I'd done so far.

I watched my brother start to cross it, walking fast to keep his balance, and then I followed his lead as the bridge rocked wildly underneath us.

My stomach churned, but we made it to the boat.

My brother bounded around the boat, showing off the work he had done. But I was disappointed; the boat seemed dinky to me.

He showed me the cabin, the steering wheel. I followed him to the engine room. My mood lifted when I saw the engine. It wasn't completed, but it was gigantic.

"A Japanese 3 block engine," he explained. "It's a good one. We have Hong Four Fingers working on it. Best mechanic for hundreds of miles."

I followed my brother to the stern of the boat and then to the bow. He opened it up, and I peered down into the darkness.

"It's a fishing hold, where they put the catch," he said.

We sat on a ledge on the deck.

"She's a solid boat, but she needs some work," my brother said. "With any luck, we can get her going by the summer."

I felt him staring at me, hopeful, expectant.

"You did a good job," I said.

"There are good people here," he said. "You can trust them. Whenever you have some free time, you can work on the boat. Just ask someone to show you. And you can bring some food and beer and take a nap. You go home at night."

The boat seemed to be sinking into the mud.

"If anyone stops you, like a cop, don't worry. You just tell him you're my brother and you work on this boat."

CHAPTER 56

Estrangement

Thu and I sat on small stools outside at a street café near my house, dim light from under the shop's awning illuminating our table. The coffee was thick and gritty, the hot ceramic cup on my fingers another secret pleasure. It was still the best time to be out of the house. All the other young people around us who had grown wary stuck inside the house all day with nothing to do just seemed to come alive.

I looked down at my arms which were stringy, at my bony shrunken wrists. The war had been kinder to Thu. Her face was prettier.

I remembered Thuy's big eyes, the shy way she leaned her head to the side after she told a joke.

"She really liked you," she said. Her voice was trilly. I felt it under my skin. I kept my head bent slightly. Steam rose from my coffee. I thought about taking a sip.

"When we learned you were caught, she was devastated. She cried so hard that night, Thanh, and for a long time afterward. And then she was, just, sad. She turned back into that shy girl, barely speaking. She didn't date anyone seriously."

A warmth spread in my chest. Thuy loved me. There had been love.

My hands shook, but I managed to pick up my coffee and take a long sip. The strong scent of the real beans brought me back.

"We didn't hear about what happened to her family right away. The sea is dangerous, the sea. So many dead."

"How did you find out?"

"About what?" I snapped without meaning to.

"About Thuy?" she said, her voice soothing.

Still, I was annoyed by her question.

"My mother came to the labor camp. She told me."

I felt her staring at me. She put her hand down on mine and stared at me with those resolute eyes. They held me like a piece of paper tacked to the wall.

"I have something for you," she said. "Like I told you."

She pulled her pocketbook into her lap then pulled out her wallet. She slid something out of a side pocket.

"Open your hand," she said.

She dropped a small square into my palm. It was a tiny photo of Thuy.

"Hold on to that," she said.

Then she stood up and put the pocketbook strap over shoulder "Welcome home," she said and walked away.

* * *

My nights were tolerable. Thu sometimes came to visit, or I went to the café with the guys or hung out at Tin's house.

But the days could be long and lonely. I didn't really feel safe walking aimlessly on the street anymore. I could barely remember that boy who ran through the markets ringing bells or playing soccer in the alleys.

My family home was now only filled with haunting memories. I walked into the kitchen and expected to smell something familiar, like a rich meat broth, a boiling carrot. But there were only empty shelves, an unused stove. I'd look in the living room and expected to see my father there, smoking his cigarette. But the living room was empty.

The house was in decay. It was damp. Dust coated the furniture. The light fixtures were broken.

When I was a kid, I was scared of ghosts. I used to lay awake at night. Every creak made my spine seize. After all I'd been through, terror was a sense I no longer possessed. But the house made me sad. I didn't have the energy for that empty space.

I walked to my room, closed the door, and opened the curtains to the light. I lay down on my bed, just below Thuy's photo, which I had taped on the wall above. For hours, I lay there with my head on the pillow, the blanket cocooned around me.

Things had flipped. Home was not home. I felt that K-3 was the home I missed. I missed the scent of jungle scat, hot fields of cornstalks and cassava, the stinky latrine, the train station down below where women stooped over in rice paddies all day. That was the real world to me.

Saigon was no longer real. I didn't belong.

I reached out to old friends who were like me, haunted by men who had been released from the camps and walked like penitents, dark circles under their eyes. Sometimes we met for coffee, and we'd sit silently and smoke for hours. Sometimes one of us would unleash a prison story we had been holding behind our teeth for years.

That offered relief, to be understood.

I wasn't due to meet anyone that night, though, so I lay in my bed, determined to wait it out. My stomach clenched. There was still barbed wire around my life. It was just invisible.

And just like all those nights in the camps when my body ached from loneliness, I reached out again for Thuy.

But this time, I only had the photo.

I looked at the tiny image on my wall closely, taking in every detail of her face. The swoop of her hair over the crescent shape of her forehead, the intensity of her eyes, her narrow-bridged nose, her half-parted lips, the soft golden cheeks. I recalled her tiny smile and the slight birdlike way she bent her head toward her shoulder, the shy luminance that I had never known in anyone but her.

Then I closed my eyes and tried to recall the photo. Every inch I imagined it so well, I could almost feel her again, her cool hand in mine, the softness of her breath when she laughed. It made me less lonely to know that she was out there somewhere, in a different world.

I started to believe she was close despite being in a different world. I felt that if I called out to her, if I pleaded deeply enough, she could travel to meet me.

Thuy, I called from deep inside my mind.

I opened my eyes on the pillow.

Thuy, it's so lonely.

The wind whipped the trees outside, their branches scratched the window. *Thuy.*

Some motorbikes rolled down the street.

The scent of the dough in her parents' bakery returned.

The funny way she cocked her head after she told a joke.

The sound of wheels from a cart passed.

I propped myself on the bed and scanned the room for her. There was just darkness and dust.

I turned my head back to the pillow but kept my eyes on her photo.

I made a decision then. I would go visit her house the next day.

I stood under the same lamppost from that night long ago, when I watched Thuy in the rain, standing on that balcony with the older boy.

Thuy's old house had been taken over by Communists. It was dark but the same huge building with the wraparound balcony. But now the windows were shuttered, the balcony vacant.

There were no stars out. The sky was murky.

I knew I should move on, but I couldn't. I was waiting for something to move me.

Thuy, I thought, recalling that rainy night.

I could see her then, the thin silhouette of her body. I remember I had been so happy to stand there and gawk at her. I hadn't been jealous at all about the boy on her balcony. I had been happy just to watch her.

I don't know how long I stood there. But I didn't want to go home.

Life had done strange things to me. It felt better to stand there, chasing after memories.

CHAPTER 57

The Mechanic

I started spending more time at the sandbar. It was a secret place. I didn't tell any of my friends in Saigon about my work on the boat. I just disappeared for days at a time, pedaling by bicycle in the early morning from Saigon. It took me an hour to get there. But the route started to seem shorter with every trip. I was drawn to the house. The lowlifes there weren't exactly my friends, but we were united by a common purpose—preparing people for their escape. It made me feel powerful to be there, like living a double life.

Each time I was there, someone would teach me something new. I learned how to hit the nails straight into the wood planks, to fix the lights and the portable toilet in the back. I spent days watching Hong trying to solve the problem of when diesel oil leaked out and endangered the engine. He was the only mechanic who could fix this problem, and that's why they paid him big bucks.

With each thing I learned, I felt a little more like I belonged. I'd deliberately taken off my shirt when I worked so the sun would tan my skin. I was happy to see that sanding the wood made my hands calloused. I would appear more like a fisherman by the time we left. Working on the boat gave me hope. Each repair was bringing me closer to a new life, the one that would begin only after I had left my country behind.

Hong Four Fingers was a jovial chubby guy named because he was missing the index finger on his right hand. His constant smiling revealed two golden front teeth. I watched one day as he worked in the engine room, sweat pouring off his face and dripping onto the metal. It was amazing that a big guy could fit in such a tiny compartment.

"Wow. It's cool here," I said.

He squinted at me and smiled, the two golden teeth glinting.

"I'm Thanh," I said, introducing myself again.

"I know that. Your brother told me all about you. This is your engine."

I nodded, and Hong Four Fingers went back to work.

My brother had explained to me how important boat mechanics like Hong Four Fingers had become. It was because hundreds of thousands were attempting to escape by boat to other Southeast Asian countries. Mechanics were a key part of the vast network of people who organized their escapes, so long as their palms were greased. The mechanics could make the tiny boats seaworthy for the ocean, so they were in high demand, commanding rates of hundreds of gold bars on the black market. Old engines in every condition were smuggled in from thousands of miles away on the coast.

"I will get this part done tonight," Hong said, "because I'm going home tomorrow."

"Where do you live?"

"Phan Thiet," he said. "It's far. Maybe two hundred miles. I just travel once a week and sleep at the boss's house."

I stood there.

"You will be the mechanic for the trip, right?"

I nodded casually to radiate confidence even though I was scared of the responsibility.

"You need to know how some things work. I will show you how. It isn't hard."

I nodded even harder this time.

I stood over Hong while he moved engine parts around, deftly pulling and scrubbing them out with his giant greasy hands, like a woman cooking a delicate meal. He spoke as he worked, and I strained to follow his instruction.

"I'm going to pull out this cylinder and then clean it up and then put the washer back," he said. I watched the strange parts move in and out of his hands as he wiped the long narrow cylinder with a rag, fitted it into the pipe, and twisted it back into the engine. I heard the definitive click.

"Now I'm going to close this. This is the shaft. This is the cam where the oil comes in."

I watched him, fascinated as he maneuvered the hunks of metal. I could see there was a kind of sophistication, a beauty in the machine itself, and hoped that I could eventually gain a conceptual understanding of it all. I also worried there was no way I was going to be strong enough to move all those engine parts, that I would actually be able to fix it.

CHAPTER 58

Farewell, My Friend

Thu and I stood outside my house, waiting to hail a cyclo to take her home. It was nearly midnight. The moon was only a sliver of light. We were standing close, and I could not deny a feeling of intimacy.

"I had a nice time tonight," she said.

She smoothed her bangs from her face then smiled in an uncomfortable way. Thu had never been shy.

"It's strange here, without Minh and Cao."

"Yeah," I said.

"Everybody keeps leaving."

"Yeah."

"Saigon is a ghost city," she said and laughed.

Of course I noticed that Thu was attractive. Her body was curvier than most girls. She was always wearing pretty clothes that showed off her form.

I couldn't allow myself to think about Thu romantically. I still thought of her as an eighteen-year-old girl and one of Thuy's closest friends. I saw her frozen in time.

"I've tried to imagine what you have been through," she said.

She parted her lips slightly. Sweat glistened on the skin outlining the bone between her dress and her neck.

"I think about you, Thanh," she said, suddenly but quietly.

I didn't know what she wanted me to say, so I said nothing.

"We all have to move on," she said, breaking the silence.

I knew then that she'd wanted to tell me she was leaving, that she was going to try and escape.

But she couldn't.

This would be my last opportunity to say goodbye.

I hugged Thu lightly and I could feel the release of her breath on my neck.

* * *

Tin and I sat in his tiny bedroom, listening to the Anne Murray music cassette on his boom box. It was late afternoon, and the rain was teeming on the window. I was more comfortable there with Tin than anywhere else in Saigon. We could sit there for hours. But sometimes, I'd look at my friend's face and briefly think we were still stuck in the camp.

It was also nice to be there because his family was wealthy.

"I'm overstuffed. Your mother is such a good cook."

"Better than Ms. Dan?"

I laughed.

"I don't really know because he didn't really have the right ingredients," I said.

Tin laughed, his whole body shaking.

I cried a tear, you wiped it dry.

"What's going on with that girl?"

"What girl?"

"The pretty one who was friends with your girl. Did you kiss her yet?"

"Oh, Thu. She's gone. I think she escaped. One by one, they just disappear."

I was confused, you cleared my mind.

"It's okay, though. It was getting a little awkward."

"She is pretty."

"Yeah. But she was Thuy's friend. Yet there's more. My group used to be so close when we were young, but it all changed."

Somehow you needed me.

"Yeah," Tin said.

"But now that I'm back, I don't fit in. And they don't understand me."

"I know," Tin said.

"So in a way, it's a relief they are gone. We cannot stay here forever."

"You like this song?"

"It's okay."

"Do you want to hear something different?"

"No, this is fine."

The rain continued to pound on the window. Tin's mother was washing dishes in the kitchen.

"Thanh, you remember that Tet. You were on stage, singing those songs in English. What was it, 'Hey Jude'?"

Suddenly, I started laughing. Tin joined me. It felt good. And that was rare.

My time back in Saigon had been like a strange dream. In the daytime, the heat was inescapable, crawling in your clothes like bugs. There was too much noise. I felt everyone was looking at me, realizing I was different from them because of where I had been.

Nights were more tolerable. They were quieter. When it cooled down, I could breathe.

Saigon was no longer the city I'd grown up in. It was a train station, a stopover before my new life. I had thought everybody else was content to stay. That I was the only one eager to escape. Then, one by one, they disappeared.

CHAPTER 59

The Boat Work

I sat with Hong on the porch of the dock owner's house, slowly sipping a beer. He was done with work for the day. His shirt was black from oil and rank from his sweat, but he seemed unconcerned. In between long sips of beer, he smiled at me. I liked him instinctively.

"Okay, mechanic," he teased. "Do you think you will get the hang of that engine room?" He laughed. I laughed too, but nervously.

"No, probably not. So I will keep taking the lessons, if that's okay."

He nodded and looked out on the water. The orange sun was sinking into the muddy waves. We heard drunk guys laughing inside. A couple came out to set up cots on the porch.

"So why do they call you Four Fingers?" I asked

He held up his hand and waved it in front of my face. It was huge and meaty, knuckles swollen like marbles. Then I noticed the loss of an index finger. It didn't stop him from being a brilliant mechanic, capable of twisting tiny nuts and bolts.

"I did it myself."

"What?"

"I cut it off," he said and started laughing hysterically.

"Why?" I asked, shuddering.

"I didn't want to go into the army," he said. "I didn't want to be drafted. So I took some precautions. Soldiers need an index finger to pull the trigger."

I took a long sip of beer. It made sense.

"But how did you do it, then?"

"I drank a lot of rice wine. So when I cut it off, I didn't feel so much pain."

We both laughed hysterically, but neither knew why.

* * *

Each season was marked by a shift in the boat building, commemorated by an occasion. One day, in the beginning of the summer, I parked my bike near the monkey bridge and noticed the sandbar was filled with people.

"What's going on?" I asked Hong.

"We will take the boats out of the water today."

"What for?"

"To check for areas that need reinforcement. Keep the leaks out. To make the boat more seaworthy."

"Can I help?"

"Just watch for now."

Later that day, I watched ten guys from the village as they surrounded our boat. They snaked giant ropes underneath it. Other guys on shore began rolling blocks of wood into place.

The guys moved as one body, groaning as they pulled the boat, lifting it.

"Let's go now," Hong said.

We grabbed a part of one of the boat ropes. I waited for the cue and then lifted it. The heaviness of the boat stuck in the mud seemed insurmountable at first. I felt my biceps might rip. But with each tug, we were lifting the boat, making progress. I looked up to the house and noticed everyone from the village had started to gather, including the women and the children. They stood in awe of what was going on.

As we continued tugging, the boat was moved onto the shore. I began to notice how massive it actually was. We started to roll it onto the wood blocks. It reminded me of how ancient Egyptian people managed to build the pyramids.

That night, I stayed for the festival. We partied on the river-bank, drinking beer and eating roasted pig and duck from a firepit. I was exhausted and filthy but happy, sitting and eating and laughing with the other guys. I listened to their stories, to the laughter of the children, to a woman singing a lullaby to a baby. Such a celebration to commemorate the reinforcement of the boat. It signaled to me that a new phase of our ship work would soon begin.

The more I worked on the boat, the more I learned. And the more protective I became of it. I helped to nail the aluminum sheet on the bottom, then cut and place wood over the aluminum. I learned how to mix coconut oil with wood asphalt and coconut skin to patch up any holes. I spent weeks doing this, tracing my fingertips along the wood, finding even the smallest hairline cracks. I became meticulous about it.

Each day, as the sun beat down, I gave my whole heart to the boat. I didn't mind my body contorting with strain, the mud all over my hair and face. Having glimpsed the size of the boat and its power, I now believed it could carry us to freedom.

Maybe it had to do with the level of devotion all the men had given to it, all the hours of sweat and muscle cramps they had given to it, or the way the villagers regarded it. There was a beauty in the craftsmanship. It transformed me as powerfully as music had.

But there was something about the boat that I couldn't articulate. It was its own being, almost alive.

* * *

It was the end of the summer. The boat was reinforced and ready to go back in.

So we reversed the intense and exhausting process with ropes and wood blocks. It was an important day, and everyone gathered to watch again. The women stood on the riverbank, trying to control children who were running around, infected by the excitement.

By that time, our plans had gained some clarity. We'd originally planned to leave in the summer, but something went wrong. I wasn't sure if the boss couldn't sell all the tickets for the seats or if the bribery cost had increased too much.

"Ready, pull."

A guy screamed, and we did the same ritual, but this time in reverse, pulling the rope to release the boat from the wood planks. My muscles were stronger by then, but it still took the whole day. But by bit we moved it until the boat was back in the water.

People cheered.

I looked at the boat bobbing, and a spasm of nausea gripped my stomach. Our escape was finally viable. We'd be leaving soon.

* * *

We started practicing the voyage. Most of us were city boys who had never boated before, so we started off slowly. I was in charge of cranking on the heavy engine's propeller wheel. It spun over twice, making a grating sound, then stopped. I tried again. It finally caught. Another guy jumped off the boat to release the rope from the dock and jumped back on board. A bunch of guys stuck bamboo sticks in the mud as leverage to push us deeper into the river. My brother Thach on the steering wheel maneuvered us out.

It was late afternoon. The heat had broken, and the wind puffed out our shirts and blew hair into our eyes. It was a great feeling to be cruising on the river, that our hard work had paid off.

We never went very far. We were only about a half mile out. But it seemed like we were in another world. It was so different and so beautiful. The water shimmered. We could see the skyline of the city in the distance. Farther down were all the rice paddies, stretching out green and pink in the sunset.

The severing of the boat from the land was enough to set me to dreaming. I started not only to hope but to believe that we could do it. One day, we would take the boat out and never return. That was the day I started living and dreaming and breathing like a city boy instead of a fisherman.

* * *

207

We were in a room in the coffee shop, behind a locked door. That's when things began to get real. It was my brother and me, the big boss, and members of the crew. I sipped on my coffee, my eyes focused on the locked door as they started to discuss the escape plan and what our roles would be. I was puzzled by the details but understood that guys who had been members of the Navy would come onboard and pilot the boat. Thach would be the captain, and I would be disguised as a mechanic.

There would be seven of us traveling to the coastal town Vung Tau, about a hundred miles away, to register with a government-sponsored fishing association. Then we would escape, leaving our dock around noon and reaching our destination before dark.

CHAPTER 60

The Day

The river appeared to widen as we traveled. By the time we made our first stop a few hours later, it became even wider, vaster. We dropped anchor. The wind raised chills on the back of my neck.

Although we were about twenty miles out, we could still see the tiny silhouettes of city buildings. There was a wide-open grassy riverbank, and beyond it Long Bình, a former military army base where the ammunition was supplied to the South Vietnamese Army.

On my brother's cue, a few of us, including my young cousin-in-law Xi, headed down to the engine room. We unbolted the shaft that connected the engine to the propeller. If a police boat came, we would pretend we had stopped because our shaft had broken and we were fixing it. We had another good shaft to use later on.

At around midnight, we were standing on deck waiting. It was so quiet. Total darkness surrounded the boat. I started to feel that we were invincible, protected by the cover of night, even though we were only twenty miles offshore of Nha Be, a small town on the Mekong.

Every few minutes, a glow moved in a circular shape over the boat and the water. It was coming from the grassy riverbank, one of the reasons we decided to launch from here.

It was finally happening. Freedom was finally so close.

"Over there," a guy said.

I walked over to my brother, standing with Xi and another crew member, looking over the side of the boat. A dim light shone in the distance. It moved slowly on top of the water. We saw a small wooden sampan emerge, like a whale. There were two pilots on each end, standing up and using their whole body to plunge the crisscrossed oars into the water. As it got closer, my brother shone the flashlight into the water, illuminating four other sampans coming in from all directions. I was mesmerized at how quickly they had appeared, by the sleek symmetry of each little boat.

As they got closer, they seemed to be moving more quickly, and some slammed into the sides of the boat. I paid attention to the one illuminated boat closest to us, the way one swung his arm back dramatically and pitched a huge container onto our boat. Next, he threw a large plastic bag. The other boats followed suit, and soon containers and packages were being hurled from all directions onto our deck.

"Go look," my brother said, handing me the flashlight. A few of our guys scrambled toward them. There were dozens.

"It's water. This one is oil," the guy next to me said. The containers were spread out all over the deck. I opened a bag and recognized instant noodles and dried shrimps, among other food items.

"Bring the oil over to the old storage below and tie them up. Then the water to the side deck!"

My brother was at my side with an oil tank while others were collecting water containers. The sampans were still hurling goods onboard as their boats were bumping against ours.

I passed two dozen heavy cans to my brother, and he stuffed them into the oil storage room below deck. My arms were so sore.

My brother had his crew shine the flashlights into the water again. More sampans started coming, each illuminated by a small purplish lantern. These boats had people in them. Some had three, some had five. They were hurtling in from every direction. We started yelling over the edge of the boat, trying to keep them from slamming into us.

There was a dull roar of voices on the wind below us. They were starting to emerge from the little sampans and climbing into our boat.

These were the passengers who had paid for their seats. They were expensive—ten gold bars a piece. By that time, even the rich had trouble coming up with that kind of money. Many had sold off their properties and spent life savings for a single family member to escape.

"Thanh, we need to check them," my brother said. He called out to the passengers, "Okay, everyone one at a time. You have to show us your cards."

My brother was referring to the makeshift cards created by the people organizing the escape trip. Each card had black ink stamps of a rooster.

"One at a time," I repeated.

A man looked up at me, his face anxious and pitted with scars. He held a little white piece of paper out to me. I turned on my flashlight, ran it over the paper, and saw the rooster stamp. I was surprised how blank the rest of the cards were.

"Okay," I said and handed back the paper. I held out my hand to help him climb up.

"Just wait on deck. Who is next?"

I moved toward a woman and a small child.

"Do you have your papers?" I asked.

They looked terrified, but she nodded quickly, handing me their papers. I confirmed the rooster stamps with the flashlight, looked at them, handed them back, and extended my hand to the boy first.

I heard voices rise down the bow, indicating a problem.

"He can come only," a man said while checking tickets.

"But my mother," the man said. The ticket checker was using his arm to elbow back the man's mother. I'd heard how families would try and smuggle on relatives without paying. For every one person with papers, we discovered two more without papers trying to force their way on. Everyone was so frantic. I could hear my brother's voice over the crowd.

"We can't let you. There is no room. You have to have a ticket."

"Show me the ticket. Show me the ticket," I said, shining the flashlight down on the man with the woman I'd just helped on board.

"Please. That is my husband. He just got out of a labor camp. He doesn't have a ticket. Please," the woman said.

I shined my flashlight on the man. His face was just like my face. He was just like me, a survivor of the labor camp. I thought of all the trouble the man's family must have gone through to smuggle him on board. Something inside of me broke. I pulled him onboard.

"Ticket. Ticket. Ticket," my brother's voice protested behind me.

"He doesn't have a ticket," I said plainly, meeting my brother's eyes.

My brother shook his head. "No ticket, no boarding."

He grabbed the man by the hand and led him back to his sampan.

All of those people were crying and screaming and pleading. We were causing so much misery down below. We had no right to choose who deserved freedom. But we couldn't take them all.

We had no choice. I reminded myself of that every time I pushed someone back onto the boat, every time I said, "No ticket, no boarding," echoing my brother. It became automatic.

Later, my brother was checking a boat. I saw a couple standing in front of him, the woman wailing, the man stoic, holding a child close to his side.

"Please, you have to let us," she cried. "We have nowhere to go."

"No ticket, Auntie, no boarding," I said, pushing her back without touching her.

We were just doing our jobs.

CHAPTER 61

Go or No Go

I watched more boats coming when I heard gunshots rang out. They came faster and tore open the sky. I saw crew members push people back into their boats. A few of the sampans were crying and yelling.

I wasn't scared. But I didn't swing into action, like maybe I should have if I was paying better attention. This same slow reaction might have been responsible for getting my brother and me picked up in the market that day so long ago, but it might have saved me at other moments. Nonreaction was sometimes better than overreaction.

I turned to see the dim lights moving away from our boat slowly. The voices stopped. The crying stopped.

But the gunshots continued in the distance.

We all stood there, confused.

I didn't know how much time passed between the time the sampans vanished and the gunfire started to dissipate. My body had frozen as I tried not to imagine being captured. I had flashes of my past, the way my legs swelled after being shackled for weeks at a time, the permanently cinched-in position of my belly, its soreness after all those years in jail. I remembered, too, the comforting feeling of sleeping in the locked down bunker there, cloistered between the other men's bodies. I longed for that small space again. It was painful to stand there on deck with our backs facing open water.

In my mind, I went over a few details in case officers needed proof that I was the boat mechanic. I'd been studying mechanics for over a year, but I still knew next to nothing. We were driving a used three-cylinder Kubota diesel engine. It was mounted to the boat's wooden frame. Maybe it would have been easier to pretend to be a fisherman.

The men who had initially repaired it were clandestine mechanics, lock pickers and safecrackers of the postwar world. If the police boarded the boat, would they detect the black market repair job?

I knew vaguely that we were waiting until the others would come on board with us. They were an ex-Navy captain who would pilot for us and others who would serve as the crew. The boat rocked, making me dizzy. A small part of me longed for the labor camp, for the security of sleeping on the tiny mat, sandwiched between two other men.

"Thanh," my brother said. I looked up and was surprised to see a middle-aged man standing next to us. I'd seen him at the café and knew he'd been in charge of some trip logistics. He was in charge of bribing the officers down the line.

His eyes were glassy, as if he'd been drinking. I had no idea how he'd gotten on board.

"Bad news, Thanh," my brother said. "The others aren't coming."

I waited.

"They were lost in all the chaos, the guns we heard. Some turned back. Others were caught in the rice paddy. The pilot was one of the men who turned back," my brother said.

The mysterious middle-aged man sighed, expressing his disapproval of the pilot.

My brother turned to me, as if he was waiting for me to make a decision.

We all walked to the front of the boat where the fish compartment was. My brother lifted the first door up. It was pitch-black. I could hear the people in there.

The mysterious man who sold tickets walked up to the hatch and addressed the paid passengers.

"Hello, everybody. I think you know who I am."

The voices quieted down.

"We have to leave soon. I know you heard the gunshots. I know we don't have everybody here. I know some of you have family members who haven't yet arrived. But it's dangerous to stay here."

There was mumbling in the compartment, the sound of short arguments.

"Right now, we have two options. The first one is to keep going. That would mean we wouldn't be able to wait for everyone to show up."

"What's the other option?" someone nervously asked.

"We can turn the boat around then take the river to another place on shore where you can try to escape. We can't take you any farther than that."

There was something about the way the guy was speaking I didn't trust. He was too smooth, too practiced, as if he'd made that speech before.

Still, he was part of the network in charge. The gunshots were real. So the options must be real ones.

It was quiet then. The silence stretched out for a long time.

A thought formed inside me.

I escaped four or five times already, and this is my last chance.

"Let's just go," I said.

My brother was silent, staring at the water.

"Yeah, yeah, yeah. Let's go" came a bubble of noise from the fishing compartment.

"Do you want to go?" the guy asked to determine if there was consensus. His calm voice scared me.

"Yeah. Just go. Just go." More voices from the compartment.

"God will help us."

"Okay. If that is the case, then we will go," he said.

He closed the fish compartment, and we all moved to the captain's cabin.

I stood on deck with my brother. There was heartbreak scribbled on his face.

"What's wrong?" I asked him.

"Nô is very close to giving birth."

I knew my brother's wife couldn't come with us on the boat.

"And it is my responsibility to meet our father when he is released."

I looked at him, and it finally hit me.

"You are not coming with us?" I asked even though I knew.

His eyes began tearing up as he looked past me.

"I don't know anything about steering a boat.'

"You are second-in-command. You will make do," he said.

I looked at my brother in front of me, my last connection to our family's past. I thought of that perfect day when we were kids, taking naps and listening to the American records. I thought about the days he picked me up from school with his scooter. I thought about how he had been the one to guide me through the boat building. In my heart, I looked to him for support. He couldn't just abandon me. I swallowed hard, not wanting to sound like a child.

"Can't you," I said hoarsely, "just leave your life and come with me?"

He looked at me for a long time. Then he hugged me, awkwardly at first, clapping his hand on my back, and then he held me tight.

"I can't do that," he said, still weeping. "You'll understand someday when you are married."

We stared at each other for a while in sadness and silence. There was no more to say. A few minutes later, he got into the sampan.

It was the last time I would ever see my brother.

CHAPTER 62

The Unexpected Captain

We stood in the captain's cabin with the trip book. The mystery man who had stayed on after my brother had left.

He put a large duffel bag on a chair and unzipped it, removing three items—a naval compass, a large copy of a naval Southeast Ocean map, and a siren horn for a boat.

These items were hard to come by. The underground network was powerful. And my brother Thach had been part of that shadowy world. I was shocked but also impressed by my brother's connections.

"This is the most important thing," he said and pointed out a long piece of carved wood we crafted recently and laid it on the deck.

"The gun?" Xi exclaimed. Xi was my cousin-in-law, the younger brother of Thach's wife. He was a sweet fifteen-year-old kid with scrappy hair and calloused elbows who had dropped out of high school. I was pleased a family member was with me.

Even the mystery man seemed charmed by him. He smiled.

"Yes, it's not a real gun, but with the cover, no one would know. You need to raise it up now and cover it as we planned," he said. Xi ran his hand along the wood, a smile from ear to ear on his face. Xi's excitement would help on the journey.

"With this prop, this boat will become a police patrol boat."

"Isn't this boat supposed to be going to Vung Tau to register as a fishing boat?" I said.

The mystery man nodded, his expression agitated.

"You will be a police boat on this leg of the trip."

An hour later, we had traveled miles along the riverbank. The wooden gun was latched to the middle of the boat, and the man had affixed the horn and floodlight on the front of the boat. The mystery man taught Xi and another man how to blare the horn and switch on the floodlight at a signal. The mystery man had bribed someone for the secret code at the security gates for boats. By giving the right signals, we would be allowed to pass on the way to the sea.

"There they are," the mystery man said.

A faint purple light was moving over the water. Through the fog, I saw a small sampan near the shore.

"Keep traveling slowly," the mystery man instructed. A broad guy was at the captain's wheel. The man went even slower.

"Okay now," the mystery man said. The guy cut the wheel but kept the engine idling.

The mystery man looked me in the eyes. There was a solemnity to his stare.

"Good luck," he said.

Before I had a chance to respond, he jumped into the sampan. We were on our own.

I stood on deck a long time, watching the last sampan rowing away, the boat slicing through the water, getting smaller.

For a moment, I just stood there, as if part of me was still with my brother. Then I returned to the present, shocked by the coldness and darkness of the boat. The wind picked up, and water sloshed on the boat.

Reality set in. None of us was prepared for this journey.

You are the captain of this boat. You are responsible for these people, I thought.

I turned toward the men on the deck of the boat.

I returned to the captain's cabin and took a count. There were twelve people, including two women. There was a couple, slightly older than me. The man was something like an ex-captain in the Navy. They were allowed in the cabin because they knew something about boats, I guessed.

"Do you know how to get us to the ocean?" I asked.

He stared at me, snarling, as if the question was distasteful. I addressed the others.

"Does anyone here know how to get us out of the river to the ocean?"

"Yeah, I know how," a man called out. I shone my flashlight on him and saw a guy a little younger than me but who possessed the weathered skin of a seasoned fisherman.

"Where did you come—"

"They sent me. My wife is over there on the other side too. I only know how to get to Can Gio. Beyond that, I don't know."

I walked toward the steering wheel. The engine was running. The guy who pulled the anchor returned to the deck to confirm we were ready. Waves slapped against the side of the boat.

"The Mekong River is very wide," the fisherman said. "It is a hundred miles before we reach the open mouth of the Pacific Ocean."

I swallowed hard. We were floating in soup.

I looked at the switch where we would turn the light on.

"We only turn them on when we are far enough away from the village. I will guide you."

I turned the key on and off. He nodded.

"Just take this boat out to the ocean," I said, "and then we will take turns."

"Do you have a plan after that?" the fisherman asked.

"We have enough food. We have enough water. We will just keep going until we reach the International Navy route where all the freight tankers go. Maybe then we can hop a tanker, travel from Singapore to Hong Kong. Maybe somebody will rescue us. That's the only hope that we have."

The fisherman pulled out expertly, his leathery hands steady. We coasted slowly, my heart pounding in my ears. The boat slid away from the riverbank, waves rocking us to and fro.

There is no choice. You can do this, I told myself.

The dark night was fluid, no beginning or end. But if we concentrated on the bow, imagining it like a knife slicing through the night, we would get through. But the fog was so thick you couldn't see what was in front of the boat.

"Okay, switch the lights on now."

The lights couldn't pierce the fog and illuminated only about ten or fifteen feet ahead on the river. It was barely better than the oil lamps we burned in the barracks. Waves crested, white-capped. The wheel slipped slightly from the fisherman's hand.

The boat started to jerk as we slid toward the right. Down in the compartment, I heard people groaning. The fisherman steadied the wheel, and the boat resumed its regular course.

CHAPTER 63

Death Traps Await

I walked down to the engine room. Xi and I busied ourselves, taking care of the tasks that I had practiced with Hong Four Fingers, like tying the oil tanks together, checking the oil, and placing the tools in their proper place. The boat rolled along slowly.

It took an hour to finish. I went back into the cabin, where the local fisherman was still steering the boat.

I curled up on the bench in the cabin in the fetal position as the engine thumped, resonating throughout my body. I felt humbled that every cell in my body was controlled, owned by the sea, when the only thing you can do is hold on, knotting yourself low to the ground in an attempt to maintain equilibrium in between fits of violent vomiting.

I was aware of the sourness in my throat and burnt rubber taste on my lips, the way my hips kept slamming on wood. I lay there, waiting, resigned, no longer even praying that it will stop.

Then something happened. The boat lurched, and my neck jerked my head forward hard, as if somebody grabbed me from behind. I must have passed out. When I woke up, the worst part had passed. I was vaguely aware of other noises on top of the boat. But when I heard the police siren, I forced myself to stand up.

I emerged on the deck then to make out the light spinning around the top of our boat. It took me a few seconds to recognize that the police siren was our own decoy. I turned to see one of our guys manning the wooden gun. I leaned against the railing to maintain my balance.

I noticed another guy on his knees, throwing up.

Xi reassured me that everything was okay. We were now in police boat mode.

I stood on deck for a while. Thach said that one could avoid seasickness by keeping your body vertically aligned to the direction the boat was traveling, in the front of the boat, and focus on one specific point on the horizon.

There was nothing to look at. Murky gray brown clouds strung like hammocks across thick black sky. Despite the boats rocking, there wasn't much wind. Everyone was getting seasick.

I waited, appreciating the cool air, and the nausea passed. Again, it hit me that we were escaping. A warmth coddled my body. I wasn't afraid.

Far away, I heard a siren. It blared twice in the same pattern: long-short, long-short.

The crew member on our boat did the same, long-short, long-short. He waited a few seconds, then he did it again.

Nobody stopped our passage. When we were well past the police station, everyone calmed down.

* * *

It was around 3:00 a.m. The wind sheared my skin. I looked out. Huge fog clouds seemed to be laying down on the river, like strange animals. The boat felt so tiny, cresting over massive waves in a river that turned out to be vaster than I had imagined.

The fisherman at the wheel was doing a good job. Even though I had no idea where we were headed, he was moving on a straight path through the waves.

The brine was thick on my lips and my throat.

"I can take over now!" I screamed into the wind.

"Visibility is poor!" the fisherman yelled back, not relinquishing the wheel. "We are about to run into some fishing nets," he explained. They were installed at the open mouth of the ocean. There were big wooden posts upon which they built cabins so they could monitor the fish catch day and night.

The fisherman instructed me to go to the front and look the nets and report back. I recalled the boss at the coffee shops telling me how dangerous the nets were. If we accidentally ran into them, they would get tangled in the rudders and capsize the boat.

That would mean the Communists could grab our boat and imprison us again.

I recalled the many neighbors from Saigon who'd died at sea. Like Thuy.

"Just go to the bow and report back," the fisherman repeated.

The waves rocked the boat so hard in the front, and I just couldn't stand up. I then lay down on the deck and began looking over. It took me a few minutes to get my bearings. I felt dizzy as the boat churned and ducked. Then things started to become clearer. The boat light illuminated a small area about twenty feet in front of the boat.

About a hundred yards out, toward the left, I saw something large, tall, and wooden, so I yelled up at the captain. I guided him to clear a wide berth around the net posts.

About ten minutes later, the fog parted, and I spotted two more wooden posts. "On the right this time. The nets are on the right."

"Go right?"

"No, the nets are on the right. Go left!" someone else screamed.

"Go left," another guy said.

The captain deftly turned the boat left.

For hours, we zigzagged through the maze of nets in the open river.

By the time we had repeated the procedure seven times, I realized something. Not only was I starting to enjoy this, but all the fear had left me.

I remembered the brave stories of the fellow prisoners in the labor camp. Tin flying the helicopter into combat, Tha fighting out in the jungle fields. This boat trip was my last chance to do something brave. I hoped that one day I could be alive and tell the saga to someone.

When the morning fog parted, I saw a town in the distance. There was the lighthouse on the sandy bank and two huge statues beyond it. One was a white Buddha, the other a stone-gray saint encircled by animals. They were in the center of the landscape, their backdrop looming green mountains.

It steadied me, seeing the familiar landscape of the country coastal town Vung Tau. But it was also humbling.

This is the last time I am ever going to see my country, I thought sadly.

Vietnam had once been my home.

CHAPTER 64

The Next Morning

"Thanh, I think we have a problem," Xi said.

On the deck there was commotion, he explained. There were two pale little waifs, no more than ten years old, standing on the deck and screaming at everyone. They tried repeatedly to make it into the cabin, but a big guy was standing guard.

Defiantly, they kept trying, their chins puckered in rebellion.

I laughed. The boys reminded me of my brother and I when we were very little, trying to get some sweets at a market stall.

"Captain Thanh, come talk to these boys," one of the younger guys said.

I turned and walked out of the cabin, keeping my hands on the rungs, happy for the opportunity to stretch my legs.

When I approached the boys, I put my sternest face on. But when I saw the younger one's face, streaked with tears and vomit, I felt sorry for them.

"Why are you boys causing all this trouble?" I asked gently.

"Uncle, we aren't trying to," said one with downcast eyes. "We only want to stay above deck."

"Why?"

"It is unpleasant down there. People are sick. The barf smells everywhere, and we are all scrunched together and can't move our legs."

"Our knees are in our chins," said the other. "The women are crying."

225

This news saddened me.

"We decided we aren't going back there," the elder one said, resolute.

The littler one looked at me then decided to fake cry for effect.

"Stop crying!" an older man yelled.

"What would be the harm if they stayed?" I asked a crew member.

"There is no room. We are all suffering."

I looked at the boys again, the way they ground their feet into the deck.

"We just want to be up above where there's wind," said the eldest. "And the sun."

"I'm sorry. You will have to return," I said.

I turned back to a crew member.

"Is there still enough food down there? And fresh water?"

"Yes, sir."

"Are the women and children okay?"

"They are quiet for safety."

I turned back to the boys. "But is everyone healthy?"

The two boys looked at each other and nodded.

"Yes, there is old puke. They cleaned it up, but it still stinks bad."

The fish compartment hatch was half opened. I looked down at it, and my stomach churned. It had been closed since last night when we decided to leave. There were many exhausted faces, and they all looked up to me. I wanted to say something but did not know what to say to comfort them.

"I'll tell you what." I turned to the boy and said, proposing a game, "You boys can be my crew now. You go back down there, and every hour you can come up here and report back to me."

My offer didn't work. The youngest began crying. The eldest looked at me with pleading eyes.

"Uncle, can we please just stay up here? We will stay on the deck and help you. We are young and strong."

The thought amused me.

"On the deck?"

"Our dad is a fisherman. We have been on boat decks since we were little. We will never go overboard."

"We will tie ourselves in with the rope."

I caved in to the boys, and patted them on their back. They jumped up and down and squealed in delight. There were moments of zero visibility, but I was impressed with the fisherman's steering. I learned his name was Cường. I kept wondering whether I should pull him off before his shift was over.

I would periodically check the deck to see my new assistants. They hadn't strapped themselves in but were standing near the rope just in case. They looked like two drowned rats.

The waves were relentless. For hours, the boat pitched, tilting on its side, and then steadied itself. Many of the people on the first deck stuck close to the cabin wall.

I worried about the people in the fishing hatch.

CHAPTER 65

Out to Open Sea

I stood at the helm of the boat and held the map and the compass on the table. Several men were standing around me, including the older guy who had been in the Navy, Hoi.

"Do you know how to navigate the sea?" I asked him.

His face flushed. His wife moved closer to him.

"Oh, well…about that," he mumbled.

I realized at that moment that the man had lied about being in the Navy. A lot of people did it. It was a guarantee you would get a ticket on the boat. Anger burned through my chest.

I pulled out the Nautical Navy map. I put the compass in front of me and looked at it, the needle bobbing in the middle. I had never seen a naval compass before in my life.

I found the coordinates on the map—north, south, east, west.

I looked at the compass. Something clicked.

Someone had drawn a circle on the map to guide us across the open ocean. I placed the compass on the circle. I remember from school that a circle measured 360 degrees. The needle would show the degree coordinates. If we were going at a ninety-five-degree angle, we'd be able to tell whether we were going west or east.

The crew gathered around me. Many of them had never seen a map.

"Woah. You can read this, Uncle?"

I made a big deal about my modest ability, hoping it would reassure them.

"Which way are we heading?"

I squinted at the map, guessing the area where we had probably left near the lighthouse.

I used the compass to chart possible directions. The soundest solution seemed to be if we went east for a while and then cut to go south. If we went far enough south, we could reach Malaysia.

The men chattered in reply, a mixture of grumbles and affirmations. This was the direction we'd already planned on heading. I picked up the pencil and ruler and made an impressive show of tracing lines for the route we would be going.

I looked at the distance scale on the map on the bottom and realized I had a problem. I didn't know how fast the boat would be traveling. We needed the speed to map out where we should turn.

"Does anybody know how fast we are traveling?"

The men were silent for a minute.

"I know how to do it!" somebody screamed.

I looked up. It was the older of the two little boys I had let up on deck.

"We know, Uncle!" he yelled again. His tiny face was scrunched in excitement.

"You do? How?" I asked.

"First you have to get an empty container. You drop the container onto the water, in front of the boat while it is going. One person stands in the back of the boat and picks up the container. Then you measure how much time it took for the boat to pass the container."

I smiled. I could only guess at what the boys were saying. But they were from fishing villages, so I figured they knew what they were saying.

"But wait. I forgot. You have to measure the length of the boat too and take it away from the other number. Do you know how long the boat is, Uncle?"

"Fourteen and a half meters," I said. "Fourteen and a half meters," I repeated, asserting my authority for the boys.

"Okay, so you know the length of the boat. And you time how many seconds the boat takes to travel past the container. And with

229

that time and the length of the boat, you can figure out the boat speed."

I was impressed and could not hide it. I asked them to demonstrate. They asked for an empty container, so I sent a crew member to get one. The younger one handed the container to the older one.

"Okay. I am ready to drop it. You go to the back of the boat," he said.

The young one ran to the back and positioned himself.

"You have to time it," the older one said to me.

I held up my wristwatch to look at the second hand.

"Okay, you tell me when," he said.

The boy ran to the front of the boat. I gave him the signal, and he dropped it in. I looked at the second hand on the watch.

"Now, Uncle," the little boy at the back said, fishing the container out.

The boys ran over to me while I did the calculations. We determined the boat was going at a speed of approximately twenty kilometers per hour. They hollered in victory and slapped each other on the back, clearly happy to make themselves useful to me. Hoi, the older guy, offered to take the helm so Cuong could rest.

I looked at the map scale and started determining how many days we would travel east before we would turn south, then how long it might take to reach Malaysia. I noted each of my calculations aloud to impress the others, but I was really just guessing.

CHAPTER 66

Third Day
The Chase

I woke up to discover I was flat on my back on the hard deck. A coat was pulled up over my chest. I tried to get up, but I was in too much pain. My head ached. My throat was dry. My eyes burned from the salt.

I steeled myself then stood up. I walked to the helm then reached for the water jug. I drank two sweet long sips. I looked out at the water. It was calmer than I remembered it was before I went to sleep. A thick cloud bank hung low on the empty horizon.

"Where are we?" I asked.

Cuong the fisherman shook his head. He pointed to a spot on the map.

"We think we are about here," he said.

I look at it, marked with the spots. He pointed out a dot representing our current location. But we weren't expected to reach that place for several days. We were supposed to go southeast for a day and a half and then turn right. But someone had made the turn less than a day.

"That's not right," I said loudly.

"We had to turn," Hoi at the wheel said. He wouldn't look at me. He had a slack and heavy face. His lips were slightly parted.

"What do you mean you had to turn?" I yelled, fighting the urge to grab him by the collar.

His wife appeared. Her eyes were kind and wide.

"He was afraid to go too far into the ocean," she explained. "If we keep heading southeast, it will be the open sea. He wanted to go south to Thailand or closer. The Philippines is too far away."

"You cannot make that decision on your own!" I yelled. "That is stupid. You are endangering all our lives!" I yelled again.

"Calm down, Thanh. It's okay," Cuong told me.

"It's not okay. This decision was thickheaded."

Hoi kept his eyes away from me, out to the sea. But I saw a faint smile on his lips.

I looked at the map again, pinching my fingers and retracing the line. My heart started beating loudly. My stomach dropped to my knees. I knew exactly where we were.

"Thanh, what's wrong?" Cuong asked.

The words were lodged in my throat.

"You don't understand," I finally spit out. "If we keep going in this direction, we will crash into this Con Son Island. I know this island. My brother was caught over there while trying to escape once. Turn the boat around right now. We must go back east."

"We can't," Hoi shot back. "We are heading for the open ocean."

"You cannot make this decision on your own. The island is not safe. We will get caught."

"Just because your brother—"

"You don't know anything. You turn back this instant."

Hoi opened his mouth to protest, but Cuong put his hand on the man's shoulder.

"Let Thanh do his job. He is the captain of the boat. He can read the map and the compass. He knows what he is doing."

A few hours later, I looked out on the water and saw a boat chasing us. My anger returned. Hoi had ignored me and had taken matters into his own hands. Now we were in dangerous waters.

The boat was at least three times the size of ours. It was bulleting toward us.

"Cuong, help me. Crank it!" I screamed to Cuong.

The engine roared and churned. We could feel it vibrating and spitting. The boat bucked and took off, faster than I knew it was capable of doing. I stood at the helm, and the wind whipped through the cabin. I felt something stuck in my chest, like I had swallowed rice without chewing. The boat was skimming the water. I kept pushing, steering toward the clouds.

The danger we faced was a shock to me then. My body just couldn't absorb it. I kept the boat steady, tugging the wheel, but I could barely see straight. My throat was dry.

In a sense, I wasn't quite there. I couldn't identify where I was, but I knew it was an old place, somewhere familiar.

"I will take over now," Hoi whispered. I jumped, not realizing he was in the cabin.

We had been running away for over several hours.

"I'm fine," I said and shooed him.

Hoi didn't budge and stayed at my side.

"We think the boat is gone. We haven't seen it in a while. But the engine cannot hold out too long at top speed. It could burn. Please go down and check it, Thanh," Cuong said.

I did as Cuong said. On the deck, I looked out. There were no traces of the other boat. The cool air returned me to my senses. I realized we had been going too fast.

When I got down to the engine room, I saw that the exhaust pipe was excessively hot. Smoke was coughing out of it. It rumbled like an angry animal. I put on the mechanic gloves and slowly eased it back to a normal state.

CHAPTER 67

Fourth Day
The Night Storm

The rain came down so hard you couldn't even keep your eyes open. Cuong yanked the bow of the boat straight into the head of the storm. I watched the biggest waves I had ever seen rise up like whales and smack us back down. He was a skilled sailor, knowing that if he turned sideways, the boat would capsize.

The crew stood just outside the cabin, roped to each other and the deck. I held the spotlight onto the water, illuminating huge walls of water that kept smashing against us. We called out to Cuong, directing him on how to avoid colliding with each new wave coming at us, whether to steer left or right.

But collision was not always avoidable. We kept smashing into the belly of waves. They physically lifted us off the ground before slamming us back down, and we all moaned and spit seawater and struggled to sit upright again.

We continued to scream out directions as Cuong repeated his maneuver, steering as the boat kept bucking and slamming. We were all astounded that our ten-foot boat was surviving, that it hadn't yet split in half.

The longer this went on, the more instinctively we reacted. The boat kept zigzagging, and we kept on leaning into the waves to warn Cuong, crouching down and gripping the rope and the railings as the boat began to ascend with the wave. I had probably swallowed more gallons of seawater in this one storm than food in all our time at sea. My stomach felt bloated, while every muscle ached.

It was not until two in the morning when the rain stopped pounding the cabin. Eventually, we noticed we were coasting over smaller waves. We all had the same dazed expressions, our clothing soaked.

I returned to the cabin and stood with a couple of crew members huddled over the map. I found the spot on the map which I could finally recognize it. I looked at the clock and made some calculations. Then I looked back at the map. My hand was shaking. I took a pencil and drew a line to indicate where we may have veered off course in the storm.

Again, I wasn't wholly sure of my calculations, but my efforts were meant to offer reassurance.

* * *

I lay in the cabin, steeling myself to stand up. It was almost my turn. We'd been taking shifts of four hours each at the helm—mostly me, Cuong the fisherman, and the old man Hoi who lied about being with the Navy. Each person was tasked with looking at the compass and keeping the boat headed in the correct direction.

Boom, boom, boom, the engine roared in my ears and throughout my body. *Boom, boom, boom*. It was a classic old engine, a Japanese Kubota. We had to keep it running all the time. Our engine was as large as a table, greasy and tarnished. But I had developed an affection for the engine as one would feel for a pet. I had gained a deep admiration for its power by standing by Hong Four Fingers for so many hours, watching him care for that engine like it was an extension of his own body. We had to keep feeding it oil. We kept it on as low a speed as we could so we didn't abuse it too much. It had taken us so far already.

We faithfully followed the pencil markings on the map. There was always one lookout on the bow, scanning for police boats or tankers. But they didn't feel like a threat to me anymore. I had begun to feel invincible, as if I'd gained strength from the deep sea. I was empowered by its shifting colors, from clear turquoise on sunny days to the darkest navy blue at night.

I had no fear because part of my soul was already dead. That deepest part of me had been left at the jails, at the labor camps. I had tasted death. My feet had been chained in the dark for days as sores emerged and putrefied. I had known starvation so bad that I scrounged on the floor for even a dry kernel of corn. I had lost Thuy, the love of my life.

Sometimes I would be steering the boat, barefoot and bare chested, my long hair flying in the wind like a defiant flag. I enjoyed the salt clinging to my suntanned skin, an appearance I had deliberately built up as part of my fisherman disguise.

I no longer felt like Thanh. I was someone different. I'd given up a part of me, the old me. I was no longer that pale frightened kid who was socially awkward, who only worried about grades. The part that was left of me was someone different. I was tougher but also colder, emotionless. I had learned to let go of my emotions, to no longer be victimized by them as I continued on this journey on the boat. Emotions were a weakness I could not afford since our voyage was a series of risks and dangers and fears. Death was practically standing on the boat deck with us. It was a strange feeling, to lose all fear of death and yet to be so deeply aware of its existence.

CHAPTER 68

SOS

We sat on the deck. The sea was so clear, so calm. I was chewing on instant noodles. The texture of the food felt strange. I had eaten very little since we'd gotten on the boat.

There was a kind of a raw giddiness in my way of thinking, stemming from sleep and food deprivation. Hunger could spur exhaustion...or courage, as waves of adrenaline coursed through your body. I was feeling the adrenaline, which was ideal for getting things done.

I didn't feel any real affinity for the guys on the boat and wasn't sure I could trust them. I learned long ago in a labor camp that desperate people showed their true colors. Most wouldn't hesitate to throw you overboard if it meant saving themselves instead.

Everything was peaceful. The only people inside were the ones in the hatch, but everyone else had come out of the cabins to gather together in the sun. For the first time since we took off, we didn't have to worry about freshwater as we had wisely caught rainwater in buckets and jugs as it sheeted down the night before.

"Here you go, Uncle," one of the younger guys said, handing me a candy.

"Thank you," I said, popping it in my mouth. It was lemon and ginger.

"I am not seasick," I told him in case that was his reason for giving me the candy. "I haven't been seasick since that first night."

He nodded as he walked away. I hadn't been trying to brag, really. But not throwing up was a matter of pride for me. I'd learned to hold fast to the wood boards whether or not the boat was still. I had become a real fisherman. I could handle anything the sea sent my way.

With all the guys on deck, there was an opportunity for privacy. I walked back to the cabin. I tossed my duffle bag on the bed and unzipped it.

I pulled out my pair of Levi's blue jeans, stroking the soft denim. I wasn't sure why I had saved them instead of selling the pants on the black market like everyone else. The jeans were a gift from my mother who was in the United States already. She managed to send them during one of the periods when the Communists were allowing the free flow of goods.

I held the jeans up against my body. The bottoms were a little too long and wide, but that was the style now. We'd seen kids wearing them in Saigon. When I got to the free land, I promised myself I would wear them proudly.

* * *

Suddenly, someone yelled. I looked out on the water, and my heart seized. I was staring at the silhouette of an oil tanker. It had materialized like a whale. I ran to get an empty rice sack and ripped the white fabric to create a flag.

I dipped my pointer finger into the mucky resin on the bottom of the oil drum to draw on the flag SOS.

All around me, people were climbing out of the first compartment to the deck and screaming. There was hope in their yells. There was relief. I felt the weight of their voices, importance of this moment.

I decided to climb up to the top of the cabin so they would see our cry for help better. The boat bucked, threatening my balance. As I moved toward the mast and the cabin with the rice sack, guys gathered beneath me, ready to catch me if I fell.

I looked at the gold ring my brother had given me before we'd gotten on the boat. The gift was to be used for a bribe if I needed it. I carefully put it in the pocket of my shorts. The boat rocked wildly as

I climbed high into the rail and tried to stand up. I pulled myself up for a few seconds, frantically waving the flag in front of me.

But the ship wasn't stopping. Everyone on our boat shared a collective sigh of disappointment, some guys screaming in vain, and then felt despair close our throats. We watched helplessly until the tanker slowly, cruelly, steadily slipped away in the distance.

I climbed back down and tried to shake off the shock of the loss. I stood in a daze, staring at the air. I looked down and realized my only shirt was filthy, smeared with oil. A button had popped off. I took the shirt off to wash it.

I casually tapped my palm against my hip. I couldn't feel it. My stomach dropped. I shoved my hand in my pocket and turned the fabric inside out.

The ring was gone.

CHAPTER 69

Sixth Day
The Tanker

I stood on the top deck, staring at the map. Then I cocked my head in the direction of a land mass at the edge of the ocean. It didn't make any sense. No matter how many different ways I reviewed our course, it seemed we still had at least two more days on the water before we reached land.

My stomach sank. Was it possible I had been so far off with the calculations? If that was the case, where were we traveling toward now? Had we been sucked up in the inlet and were headed toward Cambodia? Or even worse, back to Vietnam?

The only one I confided in that we might be lost was Cuong.

He suddenly yelled, "Thanh, get the binoculars. Look!"

I looked at his face dripping with water. Then I saw where he was looking. I didn't need binoculars. I saw a shape out on the horizon line. It was big and dark.

Tanker, I thought, the word forming in my mind, coming from somewhere buried in my past.

"What do you think?" he asked.

I allowed myself a moment to imagine making it to the tanker. Being helped aboard. Drinking clean water. Sleeping in clean sheets. Being transported to free land.

These were mere fantasies. Unattainable. But I refused to relinquish all hope.

"Head toward it," I told him.

"That's what I was hoping you'd say," he said.

I clapped him on the back, and we started laughing.

As we headed closer to the tanker, some of the men came on deck to watch. As the rain slowed, the shape of the boat got clearer, then larger.

It got to the point where we could see the deck and the silhouettes of people standing there.

But then a strange thing happened. The tanker cut a hard right and began to turn away.

"Maybe they just can't see us," Cuong reasoned.

"Follow them. Try again," I said.

Cuong cut the wheel and sped up. We followed the tanker.

"Slow down now!" I yelled at Cuong as we got close enough to read the letters on the tanker. Cuong sidled up to them slowly, gracefully. I looked down below. There were six people on deck, including the two boys. I hoped that they were safe as the wind was ferocious.

"Look, Thanh," Cuong said.

We were close to the boat. They looked to be waving, telling us that we were welcome.

I imagined myself curling up in a ball in a small cabin somewhere, sleeping. It was strange that the craving for sleep had surpassed all others, even food or water, though we were in short supply of those too. Sometimes I imagined myself back in the barracks at the labor camp, curled between Quang and Tin Buddha listening to that strange guy snore. Our sleep was deep there, merciful, and because our bodies were set and often woke us up just before the dawn broke, as if to protect us from the harshness of the cymbals crashing when we weren't ready, I often treasured those few minutes when I could lay there, remembering my dreams.

"Uh-uh. They don't want us," Xi said, nudging me.

I looked up and realized Xi was right. They weren't waving. They were shaking their heads.

I picked up the binoculars to make sure. They were waving their hands and saying *no, no.*

We kept coming up to their boat, so close that we could even slam into the side.

Through the binoculars, I saw the guys standing on the deck of the tanker still waving their arms like bird wings. *No,* they repeated. *No.*

"Too close. It's not safe!" I screamed down toward Cuong, my words eaten by the wind.

On the deck, women were shrieking. Children were crying. Others were waving their hands in the air, begging for the boat to pick us up.

The tanker was our only chance.

Please! I screamed in my head. *Please!*

My arm hooked on the railing. I lifted the white SOS flag again and waved it in the air.

"Slow down!" I tried to scream again. This time, I wasn't sure anything had come out of my mouth.

Within a few minutes, the tanker stopped its engine. Everyone cried out, relieved. But it revved up again. It didn't take long to recognize that the tanker was moving away from us.

"Follow it!" I screamed, but we were already moving.

When we got a little closer, I wiped off the lens of the binoculars. The guys were flapping their arms again. They were screaming, *Go that away! Go that away!* and gave us a hand signal repeatedly.

Our boat continued to speed up. But suddenly, without warning, the tanker turned north and started speeding away in the rain.

For a long time, we watched the boat disappear into the steel-gray sea. Our tiny ship bobbed alone in the vast sea. Any direction we turned, an inch of soft mist hovered above a clear horizon line. The sun offered some consolation, warming our clothes and our backs. But we were too miserable.

The chase had steered us off course. The open sea made us vulnerable. We could be seen from miles around. And we had no idea where we were going.

"The people are getting frightened," Cuong said. "I think the tanker says we should go west, keep going, and wait for ships to rescue us."

I look out at the sea, both beautiful and disconcerting. Then I pulled the Navy map from the waterproof bag to examine. I traced a fresh line from Vung Tau to where I thought we were headed before we got turned around. I decided it was time to turn right, heading west.

CHAPTER 70

The Seventh Day
Land!

The pure sun pierced the water, transforming the color from a deep blue to a pale shade that mirrored the sky. My tired eyes rested on the water's edge, so clear, so calm.

"Uncle, look, a bird!" one of the boys screamed.

"No, two. Look, three!" the other one screamed.

"Yes, brother, they are right," Xi said and laughed.

I looked first at the people on the lower deck. There was hard evidence in their dirt-smeared faces of the tumultuous journey and in their torn clothing. But their expressions were innocent, as if just waking up from a dream.

I looked over the deck and saw the large white-bellied birds with huge wingspans. They were squawking as smaller birds, gulllike, joined the scene.

These were good signs. The color of the water. The birds. We were getting closer to land, the boys told me.

We slowed down. For a while, we saw nothing. Doubt started to settle in. I thought I had done pretty well plotting our course, but I'd really been guessing. We could be in Thailand as easily as we could have still been in Vietnam. Malaysia was also possible, but a part of that country was controlled by Communists.

The little boys appeared in front of me. Usually, they stayed out of the cabin. But their expressions were glowing, like they had a secret so important they would explode if they didn't share it.

"Yes, boys," I said, playing the friendly uncle again.

"We saw it. There is land."

They tugged at my shirt so insistently I followed them to the end of the deck. There I saw what they did—a strip of white and green land.

"Slow down!" I screamed back to Cuong.

The boat slowed. I could barely breathe.

"Get me the binoculars!" I screamed.

Someone brought them out to me. I peered in and focused on them. My heart thumped.

Before us was a beach with white sand. Beautiful white sand. There were palm trees. Beyond that, I could see a freeway, cars and busses.

It was a fantasy world. But it was real. It definitely was not Vietnam because the country no longer had fancy cars. There were mostly buses, trucks, and bicycles.

Our boat was a few hundred meters away from shore now. Anh, a college guy about my age who paid for the trip and met me once or twice in Saigon a few months ago, and I stood on the side of the deck with our empty five-gallon plastic cans ready. We stripped down to our shorts. I was not scared. The situation seemed hysterically absurd. We just sailed this little boat hundreds of miles through fishing nets and tropical storms and unfriendly tankers, and now we were about to jump off a boat in our underwear. Growing up in Saigon didn't teach me to be a great swimmer. We didn't know how strong the currents were or how long it would take to reach shore. There could be dangerous things in the water. But none of that scared me.

Anh and I were determined to reach the tropical beach with miniature palm trees, even if we still didn't know where we were. We often heard about Communist guerrillas from Malaysia and Thailand who controlled the countryside. I imagined them emerging from the palm trees as soon as we stepped onto dry land, poking us in the ribs with their rifles.

But we didn't have a choice.

Cuong, the young fisherman, was standing on deck, waiting for instructions from me. He held the binoculars.

I cleared my throat.

"We don't know where we are. You just have to watch us and wait for my signal. If this is Communist Malaysia, they might carry rifles and take us away. If that happens, turn around the boat as quickly as you can. Just go."

Cuong nodded solemnly, promising me.

I looked back at Anh. "You ready?"

He nodded. With the other guys forming a semicircle behind us, we both climbed onto the rail to sit down. Two guys handed the empty oil drums to us. We used our feet to push ourselves off the end, tumbling into the water.

The water was a beast, sucking us down immediately with its enormous currents. Every time I attempted a stroke in the water, I was catapulted to the other side. We had to be wary of smashing into rocks. Treading water, I looked toward the shore. The white sand was so bright, the sunlight making it glisten. The oil drum slipped from my body.

I was exhausted. I tried to catch my breath. I hadn't eaten much since we boarded the boat seven days before. It had seemed sixty days and nights.

Then a wave came and lurched me forward then slapped me down hard onto the beach. I did not remember what had happened next.

I was belly down in the sand. The sand felt gritty on my cheek. The cool breeze was tickling my back. Eventually, I was able to raise myself up on my hands and wobbly knees and saw Anh a few feet in front of me. He was crawling.

There was another man on shore. He ran toward us.

It didn't matter who he was, friend or foe. We couldn't run away.

He was massive and wore a green military uniform, like the kind US soldiers used to wear. He had a red beret cap. The man was not a Communist because Communists didn't wear uniforms.

I examined his dusky face, his kind but confused black eyes.

"Vietnamese…Vietnamese refugee," I managed to croak, pointing at my own chest and then at Anh.

"Malaysia, Malaysia," he repeated, pointing to himself.

I lowered my face to the sand and I kissed it, wetting it with my tears.

We had reached free land.

CHAPTER 71

At Last

I don't know how we both found the strength to stand up. The sand cut my feet. As the soldier helped steady both of us, I realized I was hearing a swell of voices behind me. I turned around to check our boat. I guessed that Cuong had been watching our progress through the binoculars and determined we were safe, so he navigated the boat to shore without waiting for my signal.

The boat was coming in fast, so fast toward the shore, tilted on its right side. There was a big gash in it.

I was stunned. The boat I'd been working on all year, which we just brought hundreds and hundreds of miles through storms and fishing net booby traps, the boat we'd managed to keep from stray islands, had crash-landed.

The waves continued to crash over it, drowning the wood. The hatch opened.

The roar of the voices got stronger, echoing all around us. The passengers who had been crammed in the fish hatch started to emerge off the boat. They looked tiny to me then, squat women with ruined faces and children that barely came up to their waists. The men were pale and thin, weighted with drenched clothing, hair plastered to their heads. Like me, some were crying. Others were smiling. Some looked as if they were waking from a dream.

They kept coming out. My two boys. A child sprinting across the sand. An elderly woman propped up by her son. A toddler with her head pressed into her mother's skirt. Some were crawling.

They all looked wretched, wearing stained and mildewed clothes. Their breath likely stank like vomit. How had they survived in that cramped fish compartment for seven days?

I could see by Anh's eyes he had no idea either.

The sun was setting. I tried to count them, ten, thirty, until my eyes got bleary. The people spread out, forming a line that practically blocked the length of the shore.

It turned out we'd been carrying seventy-five people in the hatch, half of what we had expected.

We stood on shore, all the people who had managed to fit on that tiny boat. I noticed many were still rocking slightly, as if those days had been months and their feet didn't believe the earth wouldn't move. It almost seemed to me as a group, we were too heavy, that we would fall through the sand.

Anh stood next to me. Shards of something lodged in his bruised cheeks. Gashes marked his stomach and knees.

I continued to watch the passengers mingle on the beach. Many of them were asking the soldiers to confirm they were safe. When he did, they collapsed into a new discharge of tears. It was these raw, red faces I really couldn't bring myself to look at. Their tearstained cheeks, smiles slashed across their mouths. There was an intensity about the way they embraced each other: husbands' arms locked to their wives' waists, kids clinging to father's legs. Emotions caught up inside them like fish flopping in a net. It was just too much for me to take in, this rawness, this renewed hope.

All the things we survived in those waters were still undigested.

Instead, I fixated on my boat. It was injured, tipped on its side. Waves crashed over it rudely. I flinched as the top part of the damaged cabin started to splinter and crumble.

Tourists had gathered to watch us, to see the boat being destroyed.

"My boat," I stammered.

There was a long pause. People stared at me, confused.

"Do you still want to take your boat?" the Malaysian policeman with kind eyes jokingly asked.

Behind him, the sun was starting to lower, red purple over the bleached sand and the green palms. The temperature was starting to drop.

The waves were the pretty blue they get when they were so close to the shore. That didn't make them any less vicious. They rose up high and slammed down.

So many people had disappeared into those waters, so many beaten by waves. I pictured Thuy, how she bent her head, the way her hair shined. How violent her death must have been.

I rubbed my raw fingertips together and took a deep breath to stop my heart's spasms.

Chunks of splintered wood were beached on a sandbar. Seagulls attracted to the stench circled what remained above water. The engine cracked, spewing black oil.

My boat had been so beautiful. Now it was dying.

I watched each of its body parts go. The crumbling hull negotiated with the last of my father's precious gold bars. The wood I steamed to bend each rib with my hand. The engine just barely running, its faint beating heart. How we had coddled that engine, turning it down so low to conserve all its strength.

That boat had been our protector, our mother. How impossibly it had cradled us all.

Sun glinted knifelike off the gray blue parts of the ocean, its depth out there unfathomable. The horizon line was flat, the seas edges blurred. Vietnam, that tiny beautiful country we had come from, was gone. Only my father still remained there, trapped. And Thach, how much he had sacrificed for our family.

Inches of salty froth collected near the shoreline.

The police had started moving the passengers into groups.

My knees wobbled on that sandy beach, sourness still coated my throat. I stood there, uncertain. Freedom was precious. But was it something I even deserved? Why me and not any of the others?

And what would I do, now that my new life had begun? I thought I would cry, but I didn't.

The End

ABOUT THE AUTHOR

Frank Thanh Nguyen was born in Dalat, South Vietnam, from a large family where his father and uncles all served in the Army of the Republic of Vietnam. He spent most of his childhood and high school years in Saigon while the Vietnam War raged through the country. After the fall of South Vietnam to the Communists in 1975, he spent the next two years trying to escape the new brutal regime. He got arrested and sent to several labor camps. In 1981, he was released and successfully escaped the country and reunited with his family in the US. He went to college and earned his master's degree in computer science. He has since worked for many high-tech companies in the Silicon Valley, specializing in software development and leadership for more than thirty-five years. He is married and has two sons. Frank Thanh Nguyen spent much of his spare time reading, writing, and playing for the Mystery Box band, a local amateur rock band.

CPSIA information can be obtained
at www.ICGtesting.com
Printed in the USA
BVHW041934111022
648878BV00006B/3

9 781662 485756